BREAKING BADLY

A TRUE STORY

LOU PIMBER

CEDRIC D. FISHER & COMPANY
PUBLISHERS

Copyright © 2023 by Lou Pimber. All rights reserved.

Library of Congress - 2023905829

ISBN Paperback- 979-8-9880356-0-2

ISBN eBook- 979-8-9880356-1-9

ISBN Hardback- 979-8-9880356-2-6

No part of this book may be reproduced in any form or by any electronic or mechanical means, including information storage and retrieval systems, without written permission from the author, except for the use of brief quotations in a book review.

Editing: Michelle Morrow, M.S.

Cover Artist: Stephani VerHalen

Cover Designer: Sandra Schwartzman

Book Cover Front Photo Image: Fotojenik.com

CONTENTS

Foreword	xiii
Jay Dobyns, Federal Agent (ret.) and best-selling author of No Angel – My Harrowing Undercover Journey to the Inner Circle of the Hells Angels and Catching Hell – A True Story of Abandonment and Betrayal	
Prologue	1
Act 1	3
Pins & Needles	
Act 2	11
The Absence of Character	
Act 3	27
Sheepdogs in Wolves Clothing	
Act 4	41
Drug Lords	
Act 5	49
Dangerous Places	
Act 6	67
Dirty Job	
Act 7	87
A Very Thin Blue Line	
Act 8	97
Men with No Faces	
Act 9	109
We Create Our Own Luck	
Act 10	117
Post-Traumatic, Success-Development	
Afterword	131
Photo Gallery	133
About the Author	175

DEDICATION

Breaking Badly is written in honor of the men and women who, in good faith, uphold the spirit of The Thin Blue Line.

To the memory of Frank "Tio Pancho" Gomez & Donald "Donnie" Bertsch, may you rest easy.

My dear friends and fellow undercover brothers Andres "El Negro" Loza & Vincent "Jay" Tracey, thank you for your friendship and for always watching my back.

Mo "Pops" Reyna, you supported me like a father I wish I could have had. Thank you.

My wife, Rhonda Pimber, challenged me to finally begin writing this book in a private cabana on the beaches of Mahogany Bay, Honduras.

My kids Nicolle & MarcAnthony, thank you for inspiring me to be a better dad.

BREAKING BADLY

"If you have no capacity for violence then you are a healthy productive citizen: a sheep. If you have a capacity for violence and no empathy for your fellow citizens, then you have defined an aggressive sociopath, a criminal—a wolf. But what if you have a capacity for violence, and a deep love for your fellow citizens? Then you are a sheepdog, a warrior, someone who is walking the hero's path."

LTC. DAVE GROSSMAN US ARMY RET.

"Some of the bravest and the best men of all the world, certainly in law enforcement, have made their greatest contributions while they were undercover."

THOMAS FORAN

FOREWORD

JAY DOBYNS, FEDERAL AGENT (RET.) AND BEST-SELLING AUTHOR OF NO ANGEL – MY HARROWING UNDERCOVER JOURNEY TO THE INNER CIRCLE OF THE HELLS ANGELS AND CATCHING HELL – A TRUE STORY OF ABANDONMENT AND BETRAYAL

Breaking Badly is so much more than a memoir. Lou Pimber gifts us a real-world, real-person guidebook for living your best life as he reveals the ups and downs of his.

Risk. Fear.

Bravery. Courage. Defeat.

Victory. Faith.

Lou has experienced all of it to extreme levels.

Risk is that life-hazard that holds the real possibility of personal loss or injury.

Fear arrives when we anticipate pain or threat. Bravery is a spontaneous disregard for safety, a reaction that pushes fear aside.

Defeat is that unfortunate outcome we strive to avoid, while Victory is the reward of overcoming an adversary or mastering a challenge. Courage acknowledges the presence of fear yet moves us forward in spite of it. Faith in God, complete trust in where He leads us, overcomes all.

Those all get 'wash-machined' together when facing danger.

Lou knows. He's lived all of it.

Lou has led a dangerous life like a few others. He 'walked through the valley of the shadow of death' and came out the other side with a handsome smile. His stories and anecdotes, told with transparency, reflect his self-awareness. Being open and honest about mistakes is a demonstration of the self-confidence required and that Lou used to bring him success as a soldier, a lawman, an actor, an entrepreneur, a friend, a father, and a husband.

He demonstrates the character traits needed to overcome, then blends them perfectly with graciousness and humility. He sets an example for the rest of us of defeating hardship and misfortune and finding satisfaction in success.

Lou and I were in 'the game' of undercover work in the same era. Southern Arizona was the hotbed for narcotics-driven violence.

Lou was a leading star operator and a leading man whom I admired as my peer. All the qualities needed to be a top-flight undercover, Lou has in spades: intelligence, street smarts, work ethic, dedication, commitment to mission, charm, communication, and productivity. He checked all the boxes. He made the impossible seem effortless, yet I knew it never was.

Over the years, Lou and I have had conversations about what leads someone to success.

"If you want people to remember your name, you have to do something they can never forget."

"If you want something you've never had, you have to do things you've never done to get it."

Lou walked-the-walk. He proved those statements to be more than phrased mantras or inspirational quotes.

He made them real and true.

Life's most successful hyper-achievers have a common denominator. They excel at problem-solving. Lou always found the solutions that flipped hopelessness into hope.

That is something we all can admire.

Breaking Badly will take you on a rollercoaster. It will break your heart and lift your spirit. It will bring a tear followed by a grin.

It will tell one man's story and, through his adventures, help us navigate our own.

PROLOGUE

I was living a life of crime.

I had transformed into a criminal with a badge.

If a local gangster wanted to trade me guns and a hand grenade for his cocaine, I had them too. I was operating in the red at high RPMs.

Criminals never seemed to get enough of me, and I was addicted to the rush. The reverse undercover ops kept coming. The cases would not stop. I wouldn't let them. If Jamaicans needed to purchase a few hundred pounds to move east, I was ready because, in my experience, Jamaicans were organized, predictable, and always showed up on-time. Mexican drug traffickers looking to make a name for themselves by middling a deal and moving some weight up north or east, we had it; 150 lbs., 250 lbs., 500 lbs. No problem, they brought me my money, I showed them my product, and another buy-bust was executed.

Cash was seized, suspects were arrested, and dope was recovered. Next.

It was hard on my family. I cared, but I was on top of the world, and no one could tell me otherwise.

We became masters of street theater; every day was showtime, and we became the stars. Andres was often the leading actor, as he often initiated our impromptu undercover performances. Like a good supporting actor, I knew to make good on my lines to catch the right people's attention. Our one-take performances, often caught on video or photo surveillance by our supporting surveillance cast members, validated us and were proof of our street worthiness. The innocent people around us go about their daily lives, never knowing they were just extras in the stories of our undercover lives. The cars, planes, weapons, women, and drugs were our props; like good method actors, we took our places and delivered our lines.

King Kong had nothing on us...

ACT 1
PINS & NEEDLES

I remember my father, Joe, coming home one day when I was about eight years old, he'd been gone for a couple of days, but it wasn't uncommon since he was quite the alcoholic. He was one of those alcoholics who couldn't take a drink because if he did, he would be gone for days, weeks even. His decision to drink and leave often put our family in compromising positions. We had to move, or we'd be evicted. Sometimes we'd stay with friends.

At one point, we all lived in a garage converted into a one-bedroom home. At the time, I wondered why the neighbors were so close. I guess when you're a kid, you see things through a different set of lenses.

Aside from my father being an alcoholic, a binge drinker, and being seen on the street, people loved him when he was sober. My mother's family loved him, too. But the minute he took a drink, our lives became disrupted for months because putting the pieces back together took that long.

Jose Olivarria, or Joe as his friends would call him, was originally from California and loved the Southern California lifestyle. He had met my mother and me during his visit with family in Nogales, Sonora, Mexico, at a vulnerable time for all of us; I was just two, and my mother was a single attractive young woman. Joe adopted me. He took full ownership, putting his name on my birth certificate. I am eternally grateful for that. Joe raised me on and off until the age of eleven when he was around, so I called him dad. I didn't know anyone else. He was the son of an alcoholic, murdered father, and a loving mother.

Joe had a problem with drinking, and on this day, I recall, he had come home aided by a pair of crutches. I asked him what had happened, and instead of just telling me, he asked that I sit down and prepare myself for a long explanation. Much the same way addicts and alcoholics tell their stories using metaphors and analogies to make their point. He explained that some people live their life right here…As he pointed above my eye level from where I sat.

"I live here," bringing his hand down close to the ground.

Looking back at it now, I see he was doing his best to explain where he was currently in his life path. The conditions we lived in were often grim, dilapidated homes in areas surrounded by crime. By age 10 or 11, I had already seen a man stabbed and bleeding in the street, women beaten by pimps, and drug addicts trying to negotiate or sell whatever they could get their hands on.

My dad read books during the low points of his life. At this time, my dad was reading erroneous ways, as I called it. Part of me believes it's really what it should've been called. How could I forget it? The book had a blonde-haired white guy with a big mustache and a huge smile, *Your Erroneous Zones,* by Wayne Dyer. It was one of the books he had been given to read at an Alcoholics Anonymous program he probably walked away from at some point. It seems my father had much to learn about self-destructive behavior from Wayne Dyer.

The Serenity Prayer plaque sat on the kitchen windowsill of which I'll never forget the words:

God grant me the serenity To accept the things I cannot change, the Courage to change the things I can, And the wisdom to know the difference. Living one day at a time; Enjoying one moment at a time; Accepting hardships as the pathway to peace; Taking, as He did, this sinful world As it is, not as I would have it; Trusting that He will make all things right If I surrender to His Will; So that I may be reasonably happy in this life And supremely happy with Him Forever and ever in the next. Amen.

I did my best to read the prayer whenever I helped my mother with the dishes.

We lived in poverty, but the house was always clean. We always ate something. Rice and beans were on the table and readily available. I rarely had a sense of safety and security. The fear and sadness were apparent on my mother's face. Those emotions were unfortunately passed on to us as children. One minute we had a place to stay; the next, we found ourselves packing.

After my father tried his best 12-step program analogy on me, he proceeded to describe what had happened to his foot which had a cast and required the aid of crutches to walk. With a look of 'I made a mistake' on his face, he explained that he shouldn't have been drinking and told me he had just been released from the hospital. He explained he had gotten into an argument with a man in the street. He was drunk, and it escalated into a fight, resulting in the police being called. He reassured me and wanted me to understand he deserved to get arrested and taken to jail.

"I acted foolish with the officer and should've gotten arrested, but I didn't deserve to have the officer shut the door on my foot half a dozen times," Joe said.

Wincing in pain, he lifted his foot and showed me the visible bruising above the cast that covered the foot and ankle; it stopped below the knee. I tried to imagine what it was like to be beaten by the men I admired as a young boy.

My father stepped away and tried to talk privately with my mother inside our tiny one-bedroom home. The conversation was similar to the one he had with me, however, mainly in Spanish and with more detail regarding pins and needles being put into his ankle.

I could tell they tried their best to keep it from me, but from the look on my mother's face, I knew once again my mother was angry and disappointed. She was aggravated, sad, and seemed uncertain. My little sister played with dolls in the corner, pretending she was a princess. Judy was too young to understand.

As a kid, I always liked the police. I had no reason to fear them because I understood they were the good guys, the heroes that wore the white hats. I had seen them in the neighborhood doing their jobs, but on that particular day, I was angry at them, and I was also angry at my father. I was angry he had left us again for another drinking binge, I was upset he had put our family through the stress, fear, and anxiety of what are we going to do, but I also felt terrible in a child-like way for him. He looked defeated. You see, when my father was sober, he was such a good man. People wanted to be around him, and I wanted to be around him, even when he asked me to hold a flashlight for him or a mirror while he fixed the car or the TV, and most of you know how that usually goes. As it turned out, the incident where my father had gotten arrested was not too far from where we lived, so my dad asked if I would like to come with him. He explained he needed to go talk to some of the neighbors there to see if anyone who saw anything could help because he was going to file a complaint against the police officer for breaking his ankle. Next thing I remember, we were walking through the neighborhood three or four blocks from our home, knocking on doors, and I was right there with him. I recall him often speaking to people in Spanish, switching to English, describing the incident, or reenacting the police officer's actions. Still, I also remember no one would admit to seeing anything. Most people were shaking their heads, and some would look down at me, behind us, then at him with sorrow or pity. They would shake their head, saying they don't remember seeing anything. Even at eight years of age, I already knew that some of them were probably not being truthful. No matter how much my father apologized to them for having made a scene in the neighborhood, they didn't seem interested in helping us. I guess that's what happens when you act out and publicly drink in the streets and start fights. I read somewhere that we don't always get what we want. We get what we deserve; there may be some truth to that.

Apparently, we wouldn't get anywhere with the neighbors, and no one wanted to help. In some way, I didn't blame them. I'm sure the man they saw several days before wasn't the same man that had knocked at their door; alcoholism has that effect on people; it changes them. Nonetheless, an impression had been made, and at the same time, a decision was made by my dad to go to the police substation in our area. I remember getting there and walking in, clearly seeing all the different awards on the walls, badges on display, trophies, and pictures of police officers. My dad walked to a counter, gave his name, and asked to speak to a supervisor. We were told to sit and wait, so we did, right next to each other on those old-school uncomfortable plastic chairs. From the look on my father's face, all I saw in the distant stare of his eyes was a concern. Was he thinking about what he was going to say? Was he thinking about how this incident could affect our family? Although I was a child, I knew the reason why we were there wasn't to discuss the arrest because we can all agree looking back at it now, it was a lawful arrest but what wasn't lawful or just, was slamming a door on my father's ankle multiple times to the point of breaking it.

After what seemed like a long time, an officer called us in to meet with a police supervisor. He was an older man and a bit overweight. I recall bits and pieces of the conversation and him taking copious notes on his little notepad, but I mostly focused on the Sergeant and how he was listening or not listening to my dad. The impression I got was that this police Sergeant was more interested in questioning my father's actions leading to his arrest and less interested in the details regarding my father's injuries and how they came to be. I guess that wasn't what I was expecting to see. I was a child, and as a child, I watched TV shows and police dramas where within 30 minutes or so, a situation is resolved, and justice is served, just not in my father's case. This wasn't a rerun of *ADAM 12* where the professional and polite policeman asked questions, followed up on leads, and brought a person to justice.

I remember leaving the police station saying to myself I wanted to be a police officer because I wanted to be *the* police officer who doesn't do *that* to people. I want to be the one who helps people but also puts away bad guys like the ones I would watch and admire daily in my neighborhood.

After we left, I don't recall anything else happening again, other than one day my father and I, along with my mother and my little sister, crossed paths with the officer as he sat looking gruff in his patrol car. He was smoking a cigarette while parked along the sidewalk leading to the neighborhood *chino store--*

the Chinese grocery store. I looked back and heard my father telling my mother, in Spanish, that that was the officer right there, *ese fue el mija*. Despite this incident, I never once heard my parents speak badly about police officers. They didn't have to.

ACT 2
THE ABSENCE OF CHARACTER

I was born Luis Alberto Pimber-Olivarria in the Mexican state of Sonora. We had come to live in the United States in the early 70s. I was four or five years old. My mother grew up frequently coming to the United States with her mother and sisters. I learned living in the United States provided a better way of life because we frequented Mexico often. I had seen real poverty there, with people living in cardboard box homes with dirt-swept floors. I knew I was lucky.

Growing up, despite having a language barrier, I did well in school. I was fortunate to have had good teachers who looked after my sister and me. These teachers would go out of their way and sometimes bring us food, sponsor us over the Christmas holiday, and take us shopping at second-hand stores. *Ms. Fillman, I remember you, and every little bit helped.*

Another teacher, in particular, went beyond to help me map

out my goals. Meeting with her was the first time I had heard the word goal and its meaning other than during the game of soccer on our dirt and dry grass fields. I learned a goal was a task you wanted to achieve, and grown-ups always had them, and it was how my teacher became a teacher. She had a goal.

Television played a significant role as a kid and helped influence who I was to become. I was in the 6th grade when my teacher asked me what my goal was and what I wanted to do the day I grew up. Sadly, television is not the same today.

At the moment Mrs. Brenda Tye asked, I said stuntman because at that time, there was a T.V. show called *CHIPS*, and in the show, an actor named Eric Estrada, from what I recall, did his stunts, and for some reason, it was a big deal. So, I wanted to be a stuntman just like him. Mrs. Tye had us share our goal, which she wrote on a piece of paper cut in the shape of a star and then posted on a board in the back of the classroom close to the water fountain. Every time we went to get a drink, and every time I walked to the back of the classroom, I would see my star with the word *stuntman* on it right there. I would sometimes touch it.

There was another show in the 80s which inspired me to work undercover. It was *WISEGUY*, starring Ken Wall and Jonathan Banks. I loved the intrigue, the deception, and the heartbreak he experienced in his betrayal of the character named Sonny, whom he was investigating.

My mother and I were involved in a bad car accident in the same school year. I was probably eleven at the time. Both my mother and I sustained injuries. Fortunately, my sister was not with us that day. We were coming back from visiting my dad at an alcohol rehabilitation center that was located several miles outside of town. We were hit head-on in our '66 Chevy station wagon by none other than a drunk driver in a '66 Chevy sedan.

Coincidence.

After the surgery to repair my injuries from the crash, and sometime after I was released from the hospital, I learned my father had left the rehabilitation center to look after us. I last saw my father sitting in the living room, looking stressed as he prepared to change my dressings. Sadly but not surprisingly, it was the last time I saw him healthy and in his normal state of mind. He left on foot that night to go on another drinking binge. Several days later, crossing the street, he was hit by a truck.

The police came to our door in the middle of the night. We learned his injuries were bad, *really* bad. The Police Officer standing at our door did his best to deliver the sad news. Because my mother was still resting from her injuries, and I was sleeping on the sofa, it was my aunt that came to the door. Since my aunt primarily spoke Spanish, I had to translate for her and the officer. The officer informed us witnesses said my dad was seen intentionally stepping into traffic, and others described it as him stumbling onto the road. They were probably both right. It was a hit-and-run, nonetheless. Unknown to me then, my parents had been divorced since I was nine or so. My father's life was never the same after.

It was a loss for everyone.

My dad went to live and continued to rehabilitate in

California at his mother's home. Some people have a tough time learning from their mistakes. Some people refer to alcoholism as a disease, much like my father would sometimes describe it. Maybe it is, and I'm sure plenty of scientific data supports it. It made no sense to me as a child based on what I had observed. Yes, alcoholism can lead to a diseased liver, among other things. Still, I believe alcoholism is partly a learned behavior that results in a long list of unhealthy choices, poor judgment, bad habits, a lack of control, and a long list of broken families.

We lived in section-8 homes after my mother lost her job at a semiconductor factory. I went to a few different high schools, and we moved a lot. I hated when we had to live off food stamps. In those days, food stamps came in a thick envelope, delivered by the mailman, and to use them at the grocery store, we had to tear them off a booklet like a checkbook.

I had the good fortune of having a creative teacher at one of the high schools that I went to. It was a writing class where the teacher challenged me. He challenged the class to write our goals down along with the path we would take. I wrote a paragraph or two about wanting to be a police officer and turned it in. It was the second time the word goal had come up in my life from someone who had influence over me.

He returned it to me and said disappointedly, "It's boring. This is a creative writing class. I'm giving you a creative license to use your imagination." He explained that he wanted me to write what it would look like for me in detail, to exaggerate and to imagine what car I would drive, what house I would live in, and who I would marry while being the legendary crime-fighting lawman I wrote of.

I took it upon myself to draft a story of Commissioner Gordon from the Batman comic books. I was him solving crime in the big city, arresting bad guys, and driving fast. I had friends in all the wrong and right places. Looking back now, I should have written I was Batman instead. I am curious just how it would have worked out for me.

From that point on, I became obsessed with having goals. Inside my heart, I knew I had to become somebody for the sake of my mother and sister. We didn't come to The United States for me to be a nobody. I had to become like the men I respected and admired from far away--men who provided for their families, noble and brave, hard workers. It was in me to become a protector. Because I had bought into the idea that goals provided me a chance to use my imagination and provided me a way out of the path I was currently on.

Despite my surroundings and sometimes questionable acquaintances, I did my best to keep my nose clean.

Latina moms were well known for their uncanny abilities to pick off an unruly child like a trained sniper with a shoe or sandal, *la chancla,* and stop our bad behavior. My mother would, without hesitation, put me in my place; her chancla use was powerful and precise.

I briefly mentioned my biological father, who contributed no value to my life. *None*. He and a few of his brothers became known as notorious criminals along the Mexican border. At the core, he was too cowardly to face me.

The men that occasionally came into my life were his drug trafficking nephews, with their black shiny curly hair and fu-man-chu mustaches looking like villains straight out of central casting. Robin Hoods in their minds and seen as heroes to some family members, but complete nightmares and criminals to the core to everyone else and with a lifestyle only a mother, whom they loved but prematurely aged, could love. These guys saw me as easy bait, their little cousin, broke with no father or anyone to protect me. They were wrong; I had a hard-working lioness for a mother who guarded her cubs. Suilma Pimber was her name. She was beautiful. She had light skin and dark features and was a full-figured Mexicana. She was both a mother and father to me. She was an example of hard work and patience. At twelve, she introduced me to Jesus Christ as my Lord and savior. Sadly, she died young, in her mid-50s. Both my sister and I held her hand as she took her last breath. I miss her greatly.

I do have to give credit to my adopted dad, Joe. He was my sister's father and helped protect me from my uncles and cousins as a child. I was told he scored a few street fights with them, which sometimes landed them in the hospital from the ass-whooping that went both ways.

I had seen the shootings, the stabbings, and the assaults. I was drinking underage and riding my bike through the neighborhood. I quit smoking at eight or nine, I think! No one ever discovered I had been smoking my dad's cigarettes, one every day after school. After a long walk home, I couldn't wait to open the door with the key my mother had hidden, I would walk into the kitchen, pull open the fridge, find dad's stash, and then smoke me a Kent while watching *I Dream of Jeannie* and *Scooby Doo*. My sister had no clue.

It was an anti-smoking commercial that scared me to quit. However, I did smoke a lot of pot as a teenager. I had many close calls with the police, who gave me some grace and second chances. I appreciated them for being that understanding.

I must credit my cousin, Guillermo Romero Malpica, who lived with us for a few years. From the time he and I were fifteen to eighteen, he taught me how to appreciate 80s rock and 70s rock classics and be a better son and brother. Guillermo became a successful lawyer in Hermosillo, Sonora, Mexico. I learned so much from him; to think it all started with a phone call he made in the summer of 1985 asking if he could stay for just three months.

I had the honor to serve as a US Army Combat Medic. The emergency medical training the Army provided me was incredible. I was a Military Policeman for a bit as well. I'm proud to have been sworn in as a United States Citizen at the age of twenty in my U.S. Army Class A uniform.

I attended college, and I was able to fulfill my goal of becoming a police officer after attending the Arizona Law Enforcement Training Academy. Early into my career, I made it a point to seek opportunities to fulfill my goal of working undercover. As a 24-year-old, I made the cut and found my way into the Arizona State Gang Task Force GITEM. My score was high. The task force commanders said I was too young, but I was focused on achieving my goal. But because I was, in fact, so young and around so many seasoned law enforcement officers from numerous agencies, I quickly learned that although I had the hard skills (tactics & how-to) from my military training and experience in numerous advanced coursework from U.S. Army, my soft skills being able to ability to communicate with everyone and listen hadn't entirely been developed yet, much less my character. I had attended basic and advanced training in Narco-Terrorism, Special Weapons and Tactics SWAT, Counter Drug Training from the U.S. Army, C.I.D., and numerous other tactical schools.

Bob Proctor wrote in the book *Paradigm Shift*, explaining when your soft skills, hard skills, and character reach similar levels of growth, you experience a paradigm shift. Thus, you will be able to live a more productive and fulfilling life.

Although my hard skills met the standards of that level of police work, I could present myself well before an oral board panel of experienced law enforcement officers. My tactics were high-speed. I was physically fit. I could shoot, move, and communicate; my officer safety was on point. Let's not forget my investigative skills presented themselves above someone of my tenure, having attended numerous C.I.D. courses, and of course, I wasn't lacking in swagger or confidence.

You see, in that type of environment dealing with streetwise violent offenders, Type-A, competitive, fast-paced, and inpatient cops you needed these skills to survive.

I believed I had it.

What I didn't have finely tuned like the "instrument of warfare" I thought I was, were my very much needed soft skills. Unbeknown to me, my ability to communicate in the workplace needed work. I was still rough around the edges. I had assumed everyone around me worked to 'my level' of intensity.

I mean, c'mon, don't we all want to get bad guys, all the time?

Unfortunately, as you can tell, no one had yet had the old bull, young bull, and the cow's conversation with me. I hadn't yet learned nor appreciated that not all cops are hard-chargers. Some law enforcement officers are retired on duty (R.O.D.). Some are doing enough to get to retirement and collect a check. Others had issues at home, drank too much, divorced, or were divorcing. And others would rather be a great husband or father than be a great cop.

Slackers, or so I thought.

They were taking up space in my opinion. *What happened to wanting to go out in a volley of fire fighting bad guys? If I was to die, let it be on a pile of lead, but I would take some of them with me.* I actually used to say that to myself. A warrior's death!

My poor communication skills taught me I needed to listen better to people with more hands-on experience than I did. I needed to shut up and listen more often. I needed to learn to be intentionally humble. I had to admit although I knew a lot, at the very same time, I also didn't know a damn thing. I had fresh new tires, but the rubber hadn't met the road yet. I wasn't road-tested and inexperienced compared to the guys I was with.

I didn't have a father to mold me, to coach and teach me humility and leadership other than spending a lot of time with my mother's older brother, Jose Luis Pimber. I admired his physical fitness, toughness, and how he liked gardening, but that was it. To his credit, my uncle had served in the U.S. Army and had been a fireman for several years. He was a "functioning" alcoholic, a total abrasive jerk, twice divorced, whose kids never spoke to him. I was aware of all his imperfections, yet I often opted to hunt with him, stay at his house, fix his car, and watch him drink with his friends. According to my mother, he at least stayed home when he drank and didn't leave for weeks on end on a binge. He was the other type of drunk.

My role models had been Drill Sergeants yelling at me, *"Move with a purpose!"* My leaders, up to that time, had been superiors who never established a relationship with me and instead directed and ordered me around. I learned to move at the speed of their instruction.

There was much I could learn and appreciate from the guys who I perceived as needing to be faster movers or retired on duty. They, too, were professional law enforcement officers who had found a balance that allowed them to be good dads and good cops. I finally understood them. I most definitely learned to appreciate them later. They observed things through their personal experiences; they experienced their career and lives at a different pace than mine.

I learned and had to accept that my character wasn't up to speed yet. My character still had to catch up to match my skill level. I was still immature.

In an environment amongst hardened and experienced no-nonsense cops who have been in the shootings, the fatalities, the fights, and late nights, you are reminded of your shortcomings very quickly. I was nobody compared to them.

I met great men like "Tata Jack" and "Stevie-B," experienced gang enforcement officers who took me under their wings and guided me. All I came with was great training and an idealistic mind. Jack once saved me from lawfully shooting a machete-wielding ex-con. My abilities and training justified me, but Jack's experience is what stopped the threat. He called him by his childhood street name, enough for him to pause and then drop the *filero*.

On top of it, I learned that gang enforcement units sometimes attracted overzealous cops. Working gangs in the early 90s, at the peak of the crack cocaine epidemic, required hard men and women who were intelligent cops that had spent time either growing up or working in the hood. Men who had taken an oath to uphold the law but at some point forgot they also raised their right hand to uphold The Constitution of The United States.

The truth is, after a few years, usually about five, you start to believe everyone is an asshole except you. In many cases, it's the other way around. Some law enforcement officers think it's ok to violate a person's 4th Amendment rights and get creative with how they exercised their judgment.

I had to remind myself and my peers although we had power, we also had a responsibility to be examples. Otherwise, we acted no better than the felons we found ourselves pursuing. I never forgot where I came from, so I didn't hesitate to remind them of the questionable stops I had been noticing with more frequency.

A homie might be a total gang banger and look the part, but that isn't enough to stop someone, much less to search someone. Give them enough space and a little time, and they will provide the reasonable suspicion you need to stop, frisk, and investigate. My point of view didn't sit well with some; let's say I had a few back-of-the-building conversations with a few of my peers who didn't see eye-to-eye with me on this practice.

In re-examining these scenarios that played out then and, without a doubt, still occur to this day, I have learned that we tend to judge others based on their outward actions and what comes from those actions. Law enforcement officers are no different; we are in the business of enforcing a law requiring observation of a person's behavior. Behavior that often leads law enforcement to decide to detain or arrest. On the one hand, we say we are doing our job and deciding to detain or arrest based on *criminal behavior* and not on anything else. After all, its facts and circumstances which or that substantiate reasonable suspicion. Others observing from the outside may say or feel differently. One question I have learned to ask myself was, 'what could I or others have done differently.' We have to start with how we judge ourselves, which is often based on our intentions when making those questionable stops, but not on our actions. If we feel our intent was in good faith, then we continue in that type of behavior. The problem with that is that it can lead to unlawful stops and cases being thrown out, making us lousy law enforcement officers. That was something I did not sign up for. We can still be proactive without compromising our integrity and a person's constitutional rights.

I guess I signed up for that too, but I wasn't there to make case law.

I was eventually assigned to the State Gang Unit undercover squad. I suppose the guys in that squad had taken a liking to me. Perhaps because I was inexperienced and not too "cop-like," yet they thought I was trainable enough to buy dope and stolen guns from gang bangers. It also helped that I was twenty-four, and it's easier to buy crack cocaine from gangsters when you looked closer to nineteen, which I did.

My hard skills were allowed to work in my favor and helped improve the strength of my soft skills, thus, giving room for my character to catch up a bit. Don't get me wrong, working in an undercover capacity isn't the time to go find yourself like I might make it seem. Working undercover simply sped up the process for me. The Undercover Narcs who initially mentored me, made me earn it the hard way.

I was humbled and placed in positions where I didn't feel like I was number one. I learned how dangerous undercover gang work is, and along the way, it helped make me confident. The hazing and initiation were real, and it also made it fun to learn from. I had to develop a thick skin and could not take myself too seriously.

Along the way, we trained like we fought. Our U.C. training scenarios by design were realistic to the point you forgot they were training scenarios. We spent hours in the live-fire house creating and re-creating worst-case scenarios. A drug deal gone wrong sitting at a table. An attempted rip-off in a car... Some bad guys locked the doors behind you inside of a house. Oh, you got checked by a homie, and the bad guy wants to scrap. We trained for it.

I was glad these men and women operated on my side. "JaySo" looked like he had spent time in San Quentin in his baggie Dickie pants and oversized T-shirts covering his 9mm Sig-Sauer. He was Latino, had served in the United States Marines, his head was shaved, and he could stare into your soul with a calming demeanor that either said, 'trust me, I'm a cop' or 'trust me, I'm not a cop.' I watched him negotiate drug sales like an old pro like he grew up doing it.

"West-Side" was right off the streets of Chicago. He was a short, black dude, walked like a giant, and could bench-press a truck. You wouldn't know it unless you accidentally bumped into him, though. His pants always sagged, and his oversized Ben Davis shirts covered his muscular arms. "West-Side" spent some time running with West Side City, W.S.C., back in his day. A thug at heart who had fortunately for him met a mentor who helped redirect his life in the streets just early enough to make the cut to meet law enforcement background standards.

Even other cops were confused if they came across us. I kept asking myself how I got so lucky to be here. Wu-Tang and Too-Short played the theme songs to our lives. These guys wanted to ensure I had the right stuff, thick skin, and the balls to back up my bravado. We made our living buying crack and stolen guns from the most dangerous drug dealers in the state, heroin from Mexican Mafia gang bangers who would just as well shank you for entertainment.

We conspired to make meth with some of the vilest specimens of bikers in Southern Arizona; these guys were killers.

"There was no room for second-guessing your courage. You're either in or you are out, homie." "JaySo" and "West-Side" said this to me in unison.

By that comment, I realized they also wanted to be sure I would face the potential danger associated with this line of work with the same ferocity as wanting to live. Despite our appearances and unorthodox way of doing police work, our integrity and work ethic were never in question. We infiltrated gang sets, Bloods, Crips, and Sur 13, we went to all the rap concerts on intelligence gathering ops. We could spit game. Who else would almost get into a scrap with one of the homies of the opening act to ICE-Cube's Westside Connection crew? I did. It was 1994-95, and we were under cover…

They didn't know that they were actually doing me quite the favor because that's where I wanted to be. No matter how much they hazed me, embarrassed me in front of low-level drug dealers, or made me walk back at night in an unknown town. I was armed and looked like the gangster your mother warned you about without my credentials. They forced me to figure it out. I was glad the local cops never stopped me from walking while Mexican. *Ice-T did say, after all, "I am a nightmare walking, psychopath talking, king of my jungle just a gangster stalking..." At least, that is what I said to myself.*

I learned that being undercover involves you becoming accustomed to pushing past your fears, working outside the box, having the trust of your partners, a sound operational plan, a solid cover, and a tactically proficient rescue team. It required courage and creativity as well. Sometimes, we acted as our very own rescue. We carried no radios or badges and wore no body armor.

I realized that solid cops and a good op plan could make up for poor leadership. I even learned, among other things, how to cook crack-cocaine in a hotel with a suspect who I named "Tupacks" because he looked just like the real thing. He had game, girls, and was posted in a hotel right off I-10. People would line up for him; they'd give their children to get his homemade delicacy, also known as cookies, nuggets, and rocks. Unfortunately, his was the life of a westside player and sadly he later learned heaven has a ghetto.

ACT 3
SHEEPDOGS IN WOLVES CLOTHING

I served in the State Gang Task Force for a couple of years and was later transferred to the elite HIDTA drug task force. High-Intensity Drug Trafficking Areas (HIDTA), a program created by Congress with the Anti-Drug Abuse Act of 1988, assists Federal, state, local, and tribal law enforcement agencies operating in areas determined to be critical drug-trafficking regions of the United States.

Things got very real, real fast. I had accomplished another goal—the chance to work with the best of the best as an undercover drug operative. Like *Tony Montana, the world was mine.*

Things don't always go as planned, though.

The truth is, like many other industries, cop work also suffers from poor leadership. Men and women "rise" into leadership not because they wish to lead by example or teach their subordinates but for self-serving reasons.

Some leaders are there to police the police, earn more stripes, and accolades on the backs of their men and women. Some were looking to keep their jobs and willing for you to lose yours so they didn't have to. There were supervisors too afraid to take chances even though they weren't the ones going into harm's way. They took "their chances" vicariously through us. When you take controlled chances, you learn from them; to some commanders, a mistake meant failure, not an opportunity to gain experience.

I got to the HIDTA Task Force, and I had the chance to collaborate with a good friend of mine "Vincent Johnson," Aka: "Vincent-T," "Jay."

"Jay" was a blue-eyed, white boy with blonde braids, tattoos, and a hood-like attitude. He was a US Army Veteran and MP School Honor Graduate—the proud son of a US Army Vietnam Veteran, whom he was named after.

"Jay" was a real squared-away guy and in impeccable shape. I had never seen a white narc like him work in this type of undercover world before. I'm not so sure anyone at HIDTA had either. He bought more crack-cocaine from blacks than the black UC Narcs in our unit. He was so convincing a well-known black gangster disciple chose to take the stand in his defense and testify, "I ain't never sold to no white boy…." Surveillance footage proved otherwise. "Jay" was a natural-born leader, a thinker, and a hard-working father to a beautiful little girl. True to his Honor Graduate form, "Vincent-T, aka; Jay," bounced back like the leader he was and always will be. Undercover work can be hard on a family, and it took its toll on "Jay." My dear friend went through a horrible divorce.

People like to think undercover work is sexy, even glamorous. My good friend and fellow Undercover Operative, "Jay-Bird" Jay Dobyns, once described, "It's a vomit-covered scab filled with women with tits that hang like socks with baseballs in them…"

I was exposed to great people, federal funding, and a chance to work on more prominent cases. I had access to three-letter agency technology, high-tech surveillance equipment, aircraft, and a fleet of undercover vehicles. It's where I learned the term little cases, little problems. Bigger cases, bigger problems, which means if you want to have small problems and a stress-free career, keep your cases small, don't make any waves, and no one will ever know your name. But, if you want to make an impact and get the lion's share of the cases and the glory, do what lions do, take on bigger prey, work longer hours, and take more calculated risks. I also knew going into a unit like that meant that I had to earn my spot and the trust of my fellow Narcs once again.

There was no welcoming party. I wasn't greeted with open arms from everyone. One guy, who I'll call "Super-Narc," and another whose work I admired, known as Don by far, were the most unwelcoming, condescending, and rude without any real reason other than perhaps my reputation from the State Gang

Unit UC Squad. I can't blame them. One hundred percent of my confidence came across as cocky. Truthfully in comparison to Don or "Jay" specifically, I wasn't much of a Narc. Don had pushed the envelope as a UC. He overcame many personal challenges and obstacles in his life. He raised the bar and set the standard for guys like me to follow.

Don and my good friend "Jay" had done excellent work well before I had gotten there, and their reputation was one to be respected. I was with real players here. At HIDTA, we had bigger fish to fry, larger targets, players in moving dope across state lines, the US/Mexico border, and ties to national drug traffickers. It was ripe for the taking, and I had a chip on my shoulder.

The RODs worked there, with plenty of retired-on-duty types, but they performed great at providing surveillance and cover. They were detail oriented and patient. The cops who'd rather be awarded dad or husband of the year were evident, too; they were usually assigned to support financial crimes. They got good at taking money from bad guys and following their money trail; once we went in and identified their schemes, their sources, their ways, and means is how we investigated them, and it was their lack of ethics and morality that got them arrested. I learned to appreciate them all.

The Racketeer Influenced and Corrupt Organizations Act of 1970 (RICO) was often the tool used to charge a suspect. To violate RICO, a person must engage in a pattern of racketeering activity connected to an enterprise. The law defines thirty-five offenses constituting racketeering, including gambling, murder, kidnapping, arson, drug dealing, and bribery. Significantly, mail and wire fraud are included on the list. The financial squad seized money, cars, houses, and even the family jewels. Financial Investigators found their niche and earned their keep until one of them decided to embezzle nearly one million dollars. He made us all look bad.

Every drug trafficking tip came our way, it seemed, feds, state, and local needed a UC. We were it.

Before I knew it, I was knee-deep with "Chuco," a Compton Varrio 113th Street (CV113) bona fide gangster. An undercover drug case with a legit California two-time loser, one more strike, and he stood out: a veteran, a Vato who led me to cocaine being moved into California from the Arizona/Mexican border and crack cocaine being sold locally by his brother. Chuco and the activities of his crew gave way to us discovering legit drug smugglers pushing weight from their contacts in Mexico and then north via the Sonoran desert. They had no idea of what was about to happen to them.

Drug dealers will trade their crown jewels, their family heirlooms, and even their children to make a profit.

That's not even the crazy part. Imagine going into a house where you know kilos of cocaine are being chopped up and stepped on within the proximity of baby formula and a baby nearby. Or can you picture the anticipation of waiting to meet with members of the Huns, a notorious motorcycle gang in a shithole hotel because they believe you're "the Mexican guy" who can provide them with barrels of red devil lye their cooks need to make methamphetamine; what a rush. Lye, we were going to obtain from the state-controlled substance laboratory. As it turns out, the primary meth dealer was the female who brought her gun-toting-long-haired-psycho-looking-bikers and her baby to a drug deal.

It's the meth dealer, a once formidable athlete turned biker, now meth user and cook. He had unwittingly turned informant and introduced me to them. Along the way, he wants to fight me and then jumps out of my car because he's worried there are cops under the hood of my car. He had no idea, or did he? I'll call him "Cowboy."

Who else gets to the party, drinks with criminals, and then drives a car loaded with drugs and money with fictitious Mexican plates? I was getting paid for *this*, and I was addicted to the rush, the strip clubs, the late-night warrants, the drug deals, the cash on hand, undercover credit cards and identification, lying, and committing crimes all under the color of my authority. I was addicted to the adrenalin, the high, and the danger we were a part of daily.

All the near hits and the misses, yet I was not about to miss an opportunity. I had no downtime, nor did I want it. I wanted more. I was married to a woman I didn't know well. I was also a father to a five-year-old daughter and a three-year-old son. Part of me didn't care; because I was a Sheepdog, a sheepdog in a wolf's clothing protecting the innocent, the weak. Ret. US Army LTC. Grossman, 75th Ranger Battalion, wrote in *On Killing that* I was amongst *the protectors who could bring violence and harm, but never to the sheep.*

I just wanted to become someone others could be proud of.

The drug war is a business on both sides, except one ends in prison. I stand corrected. I've seen it happen on both sides. Through my academic experience and research, I read quite a bit about the business within the illegal drug trade. I learned as an Undercover Agent that I had an army of resources available— from military intelligence to the latest weaponry, surveillance equipment, aircraft, and drugs. With these tools, I could legally seize money, assets, and resources from the drug dealers whose function was to buy drugs from suppliers and move it across the country. I could also pass myself off as a drug trafficker, not just a buyer seizing drugs and assets but as a drug dealer with the law on my side.

If I wanted to attack their pockets, I had to become the supplier. Far better undercover narcs before me had done this several years back. I wanted to do what they had done. I wanted to bring back the Reversal Op. Here was the challenge. It has led to corruption in the past and can be politically unfavorable. My advantage was that I had earned the trust of a top-notch prosecutor who had in her past prosecuted New York mobsters and had a big pair of balls of her own. She had a reputation for making grown men cry. Imagine *Beth* from *Yellowstone*. Now picture her as a law enforcement prosecutor and on our side. I successfully briefed her on my intentions on how I wanted to pass myself off as a supplier of large amounts of cocaine and marijuana. I had become a "criminal" like my cousins without joining their band of crooks, *mal vividos*. I had a new partner, an absolute natural who went by the street name "Andres el Negro." He was a hybrid, a Mexican American Chicano with Native American Yaqui lineage, a real tough guy with braided black hair. Andres had served as a US Marine in a Marine Expeditionary Unit, a self-admitted bully.

The kind of Narc you could trust with your life but not with your wife.

Andres and I had earned the head prosecutor's and her advisors' trust. On top of that, we had gotten the buy-in from our supervisors, which we so badly needed. Reverse-sting operations had many working components and were considered highly controversial and extremely dangerous. We were going to be hitting the bad guys in their pockets, and we had access to top-level confidential informants from three letter agencies if we needed them.

By this point in my undercover career, I had assumed various identities and earned different nicknames like, "Chino," "Gallero," or "Potrillo."

Without going into the details, I can tell you with the support of our highly competent intelligence, surveillance, and cover teams, Andres and I successfully orchestrated numerous marijuana and cocaine reverse sting ops. We seized lots of money, cars, homes, and cash.

Picture two Latino males sipping on some 40s in their Firebird at a local self-serve car wash striking up a seemingly "random" conversation with a few girls. The girls couldn't help but notice the puppy pit bulls we had with us that "Andres'" cousin was supposedly selling. We were undercover narcs rolling with puppies "for sale."

Who would suspect cops would do something like that?

We did it, leading us to one of our first self-generated reverse sting ops we successfully prosecuted. These girls were well-connected, and once they learned we were "well-connected," too, they happened to be more than happy to introduce us to guys with money looking to buy large sums of marijuana. The first intro they made led us to a wanna-be mafioso, a flake with no real access to cash, a *bajador*. He was a jacker - a rip-off artist. We had to look out for those types, as well. They were perhaps the most ruthless and dangerous. We dealt with him later.

They later introduced us to a guy I'll call "Angelito," he was a local mafioso. Our background investigation verified "Angelito" was legit, with a prior conspiracy to sell a controlled substance case behind him. There was no way he could say we ever entrapped him.

Don't worry. It wasn't our style to bring charges on a couple of girls just wanting to impress two dudes they had just met. We quickly cut those girls out of the picture.

"Angelito" had been doing dirt for some time, and now we were *doing dirt* together, except he was in my element. Per our standard operating procedure, we ran it by our legal counsel, and she gave us the green light.

It was a go.

Our initial meeting with him went as planned, he felt us out, and we felt him out. We rolled up in my Ford Explorer with Mexican *placas* (plates). We sold "Angelito" on the idea that I was a Mexican national and my *primo,* "Andres," was my right-hand man—the muscle.

Back in 1999, that close to the border weed was going for $425-$500 a pound when purchased in large quantities. He wanted to move 450 pounds of our sticky icky out east. We knew he stood to make about $75-$100 per pound in profit, possibly more. Without a doubt, It was going to some east coast middlemen who were willing to pay $500 to $600 per pound, and in return, they would transport and sell it to east coast buyers for up to $800 per pound. So, we drove a hard bargain and settled on 450/lb.

Here was the game; Andres was my English-speaking cousin, and I was the Mexicano connected with direct ties to my Mexican smuggling family. He was sold. We had already brought him a 'photo'— the street term for a sample. I guess back in the day, dudes like us would bring an actual polaroid picture of a load of weed. In my time, we were authorized to obtain and walk several pounds of marijuana for them to inspect and sample. It was the risk we took and the cost of doing business for the greater good.

On the day of the op, we briefed the County SWAT cover team, high-speed dudes. The attitude of this team was different. It was the type of department where they knew their position in SWAT wasn't guaranteed. They had to earn it every single day. Every warrant they served, every vehicle take-down, every street jump meant they were still being selected. Their culture was different, and they were humble. The admiration was also mutual.

The plan went like clockwork; we arrived at "Angelitos" house with all units ready. A typical middle-class home with a large open carport, an old broken-down car parked in the open dirt front yard, and a chain link fence secured the house and kept the Dobermans from running out. "Angelito's" blue, newly painted, lifted 80s Chevy Blazer and a couple of newer model Buick Regals were parked in front of the home. He and three other dudes greeted us, ready to offload bales of *mota*, that were delivered. Chicanos who, at any moment, would happily take our lives and our drugs if we gave them the opportunity to do so. We weren't stupid. We were highly trained and professional "drug dealers," too.

I made it a point to ensure that they knew we didn't have the product with us, and they wouldn't see any more until we saw their paper (the money), all of it, *todito,* nothing less; you do the math.

Orchestrating deals like these requires many moving parts. Authorization from higher-ups, pre-operational briefings, background checks, intelligence support, a cover team, SWAT, aerial surveillance, everything to help mitigate the loss of life. By no means were we there to fight fair. Like most drug dealers, "Angelito" had a big ego and did some posturing of his own, bringing out a fancy AK-47 which he happily loaded a full magazine into the magazine well, then he proceeded to show it to us. My *primo Andres* played along but was smart enough to act impressed and asked to check it out, and "Angelito" proudly handed it over.

Andres, on the other hand, took the magazine out, cleared it, then lay on the sofa right next to us after admiring it some more.

"Angelito" earned himself another charge, the use of a firearm in the commission of a felony.

I didn't like stacking any more charges than I had to, but he asked for it. Some people *just love* doing time.

SWAT was sweating .223 bullets listening in. I'm sure our boss was, too. At any moment, this meeting could turn ugly. The sound of an AK-47 racking a round is distinct. It was our boss's job if things went horribly wrong, but our lives were at stake. Things get very real and fast too. They always did.

I was there to allegedly bring a load of marijuana that had been fronted to me, according to my cover. It was advanced to me by my "family" in good faith that I would come through with the money. I wanted nothing to do with having a beer with them or talking shop beyond what we agreed to be there for.

Andres played along and sipped on the beer handed to him until the money was brought out, not in envelopes, as you might see in movies. There were no checks to write, just a large Safeway paper bag filled with the 20s, 50s, and C-notes from the master bedroom of the home.

Things get real when money shows up. It's like when the bill is brought to the table after a long dinner and several rounds of drinks. It gets quiet for a moment, except in a high-stakes drug deal, thoughts like freedom, prison time, dreams of fancy dinners, hookers, cocaine, and booze runs through the mind of even the most tenured *traficante*. It was a rush, and I was on it.

My heart was beating like I was in a sprint, doing my best to fight tunnel vision, the what if's. Once I saw the overt act of bringing out the money, I motioned to Andres to check it. Our conspiracy was complete. I stepped outside to call my "driver" in with the load of marijuana *y se acabo*. It was over... for them.

My primo "el Negro" stepped out to 'ask me a quick question.' That's when the County SWAT team rolled up. A contingent of them taking the three eager extra hands outside into custody, the primary arresting team entered the home, seizing evidence, securing the residence, and taking "Angelito" into custody.

"Angelito" lost over two-hundred thousand of someone's money and his freedom. The disappointment on his face was priceless. How could we have done that, or rather how could he have done this? When he was done, "Angelito" was returning to the penitentiary, and we were going home to our kids, families, dogs, and hobbies.

My cousin and I got into my car and drove away like nothing ever happened, observing everything unfolding in my Ford's rearview mirror.

Other ops went down similarly. Sometimes we were dealing. Sometimes we were buying. We bought pounds of Mexican powder brown heroin to keys of cocaine. We were living it up, taking souls like we did "Diablitos."

"Diablito" had been supplying us coke from a direct source, so he says. Based on the price, he was probably telling the truth. Because we had intelligence on who he was, and he wasn't going anywhere anytime soon. We let him walk after each sale, meaning we wouldn't arrest him yet.

Remember that prosecutor I told you about? She had us arrange to pick him up. It was very low-key. He was brought to a nondescript downtown building where we "betrayed" him, badges in hand.

We took our chances breaking cover. It wasn't often—only when we knew we had bigger players to meet or if the benefit outweighed the risk. It was all part of the games we played—street theater.

"Beth," the prosecutor gently reminded him he would never see his children grow, his daughter would end up calling another man dad, and his wife would call this guy daddy. He sang like a bird.

ACT 4
DRUG LORDS

"Chuy" refused to sing like the bird he was even after he blew up my phone for three days straight. He was begging me to bring him three kilos of cocaine, of which I had already shown him a sample a few days prior.

As it turns out, bad guys forget we undercover narcs take a day off or two. I had a family. My daughter needed her daddy to read books, help with her homework, and gossip about her day with her friend Jordan. My son needed me to wrestle, play hulk vs. spider-man with him, help volunteer coach, and bring bubble gum for the team during his little league baseball games. I wanted to "be off," but I couldn't. There was no way I would be like the RODs I saw at the office.

Bad guys did terrible things 24 hours a day, seven days a week.

I had to answer that call yet still hold my ground, "Chuy, I'm fuckin' busy, bro. I'm out of town!" and hung up. Putting off a bad guy and saying no, not right now, was hard, but it became easier as I matured into the drug game. Yet, guys like "Chuy" would be in my head the whole time I was with my family. What if they go with another drug dealer, a real one, and I never hear from them, much less arrest them?

A few days later, "Chuy" got his cocaine. Sources told me he stood to make a massive profit after he handed over *la coca* to his New York Jamaican contact who was funding the buy. "Chuy" was the middleman, the broker.

I also knew the Jamaican Bobo was piecing together a larger coke load to move east. He was undoubtedly sitting on more money than just the three keys that "Chuy" told him he could get through me.

I met "Chuy" in the parking lot of a local eastside supermarket and brought him his coke in complete *mafioso* fashion. I also made it rain cops on "Chuy" that day. I also knew the financial squad pursued Bobo and the Jamaican money connection.

"Chuy" didn't say a damn word.

I had the pleasure of working with a legendary Undercover Narc who went by "Pancho." To me, he was "Tio Pancho." You would never guess he was a *chota* (a Narc). He was short in stature and wore polyester wrangler jeans and cowboy boots. He had a beer belly, thinning black hair, and a small ponytail. He attained the rank of 1st Sergeant in the US Army in his youth.

Would you believe that sometimes my "Tio Pancho" wouldn't carry a gun into a drug deal?

He said the dopers of his era didn't do that. "You'd get federal time for that schet!"

According to the bad guys we met along the way, he was a *very* well-connected drug dealer. As far as they could tell, he only spoke Spanish. I played the role of his nephew, living in the states and going to college.

One day, based on a tip we had gotten, I cold-called a man I'll call "Judge." It was suspected he had been laundering money and helping to facilitate the storage of large shipments of marijuana and possibly cocaine. We didn't know where.

The call went something like this:

"Hello, it's the Mexicans…"

The Judge immediately bit.

I told him a very reliable person had informed me that he could be helpful. It was all it took.

He asked what I was moving.

I told him Christmas trees and the season was upon us.

He requested I call him later that evening.

As far as we were concerned, he was probably doing his own checking around, his due diligence. Tracing our phone number and the name I had dropped. We had that covered too. But I can't share those details with you. As planned, we called him later that night and agreed to meet.

The old man wanted to meet at a local private jet hanger and talk to us a few thousand feet up in the air where we couldn't be surveilled. He was nuts.

I had watched *Scarface* plenty of times and wasn't about to be tossed out of an airplane. I said no. As it turned out, we met of all places at a Dunkin Doughnuts. Cliché, I know. Nonetheless, we agreed.

"Judge" was an older man, in his 60s, originally from Chicago, Illinois. He stood 6'2" with thin, gaunt facial features. He spoke with a heavy Chicago accent, and as it turned out, he was at some point a lawyer and boasted about being a judge. Although, that part was not confirmed. His greedy modus operandi was that he would rent townhomes to drug traffickers looking to use them as midpoint locations as stash houses for marijuana or cocaine until buyers were identified and the drugs were moved. He wanted to play, and we were the biggest game in town.

His elderly mother had left him an entire estate of high-end rental townhomes that no one would ever suspect a few had been "rented" to drug smugglers. He, his wife, and their teenage daughter lived in a custom home in the high-end area of the foothills north and east of the townhomes. He had an older daughter who had already moved out.

After bringing drugs north of the border, one of the biggest challenges for drug smugglers was finding a place to store their product temporarily. At the same time, the buyers were identified, and their drivers were set up to move their precious produce north, east, or west.

Storage facilities were not very trusting and leaving a loaded car in a parking lot also raised challenges and concerns for smugglers.

The 'ol "Judge" had found a solution to a problem and had been doing this for some time. A real capitalist. He suggested we draft, according to him, "air-tight" fictitious lease agreements prepared by him through his LLC, then signed by us. He said he wanted to cover himself in the event of an audit. He even provided me with a copy for my records.

Imagine that.

We wanted to ensure he was as connected as he said. Surveillance techs and gadget-guys from our unit, using the latest in technology, came in and wired up the houses with video and live audio feed. It was on.

Our exorbitant rent was paid in cash, half now and the rest once we ensured our loads left the townhomes without incident. At least that was our story, part of our agreement and an element of our conspiracy.

Our financial crimes investigators were on it as well. Researching our target's finances and business dealings to identify how many homes or businesses our target possibly owned and if any of the suspected stash houses in the area belonged to him or his business. Things began to escalate, "Judge" liked that we were clean and didn't attract too much attention either. He kept asking when we would have our first load and was hoping I could give him a little something to smoke on.

I knew better than to allow a criminal like him to dictate the direction and pace of my investigation. I also knew he could have been testing or setting us up. We were clean and didn't attract too much attention after all. Never underestimate a determined criminal. It was decided that we would put our dope where our lease was, and so we loaded the house with a few hundred pounds of marijuana.

The "Judge" didn't know we were coming, of course.

We parked a Dodge Caravan fully loaded with weed in the garage, and for added good measure, we brought along a few shady-looking characters to pose as the drivers.

I then called "Judge" on over and, surprise, "We got weed!"

His eyes widened, and his mouth watered.

As the world would turn and a few days later, he arranged a dinner meeting at a local Mexican restaurant. His intention was to get even more involved in our enterprise. Both "Tio" and I attended. So did our cover team, who sat close by.

"Judge's" wife was intrigued by us both.

Their 18-year-old daughter also tried to cut herself into the deal. She said she had never met a *drug lord* before and offered to become my "Tio's" accountant. She later became involved in the weighing of the dope and the counting of the money.

I could not believe what my eyes were seeing, and my ears were listening. This whole upper-class family was corrupt.

At the end of the meeting, my "Tio," being the class act and drug lord he was, refused to allow them to pay for dinner. He slid me the bill, and I picked up the tab. *That is what the junior Drug Lord was for.*

Long and short, we played this drug dealing soap opera with "Judge." We did everything possible to cut his wife out, but she kept finding her way in.

"Tio" finally flat out told them he wanted nothing to do with the kid.

Of course, true to character, after what they did say I translated, and every time "Tio" looked at me and asked, "Que dice?" (what did they say?). It reached a point where we ultimately unleashed the hounds on "Judge."

SWAT took him down hard in front of his favorite northeast side affluent coffee shop. We wanted him to know flash bangs and public area arrests weren't just for the homies on the southside. At the same time, the financial squad served a warrant at his home. His wife was charged as a co-conspirator, but we left the daughter alone. We seized everything we had articulable reason to believe had ties to his criminal enterprise. His homes, cars, and accounts, including every town home we had arranged to rent. If he had even looked at one of his townhomes and he said that it was purposely vacant and available to us, we took it too. We could never find his airplane; maybe, he didn't own one.

"Judge" went to prison briefly, and the wife pled out to a lesser charge. They were financially ruined and broken by the time he got out. Sadly for his family, he died a few years later, but at least he was a free man.

ACT 5
DANGEROUS PLACES

The reverse undercover ops kept coming. The cases would not stop.

I wouldn't let them.

Flaco was one scary-looking lanky villain, he had evil in his eyes and MS13 tattoos on his body. Someone rumored that he was wanted in his home county of El Salvador for killing a cop and was possibly fleeing Mexican law enforcement authorities for unknown crimes.

For us to verify this, we had to take him into custody. Since he was known for selling black-tar heroin by the pound, we wanted to permanently rid him from our community and send him on his way. We got word that my go-to reliable, confidential informant could set up a chance meeting, but Flaco didn't bite.

Our surveillance units reported he slowly rolled into the diner parking lot where he was to meet us. Something had spooked him. He sat in his car for about five minutes and took off.

Was it the side of town we chose? Did he spot our surveillance? Or he had counter-surveillance himself. We didn't know.

He might be a criminal, but to be a good criminal, you had to have good intuition, and, on this day, his spidey sense was right. He was about to meet a narc. Like a good career confidential informant my guy was, he kept his nose to the ground and sniffed out another random chance opportunity to meet my Salvadorian suspect.

My source learned Flaco was in a bind and needed to offload some product fast. Heroin, especially black tar heroin, in large quantities, is hard to come by and sometimes tricky to stash. It was dirty and often came wrapped in cellophane that was probably smuggled covered in motor oil, inside engines, car tires, or worse a dead body. Heroin typically emits a very strong ammonia-like odor. Then, there was the problem that heroin junkies were uniquely adept at theft.

Flaco either was buying this costly product and needed to get his return on investment as soon as possible or someone had fronted him the dope and needed their money quickly. Being a drug dealer tends to increase your level of urgency. Like any drug dealer, the risk of losing someone's product often comes with fatal consequences.

We set up a meeting. Our C.I. arranged for Flaco to meet him casually in a grocery store parking lot. Here's where the street theater came into play.

My cousin, Andres, and I happened to be in the area and walking up to our C.I. as he spoke to Flaco. We met briefly. The C.I. made an intro and told Flaco that "Gallero," referring to me as *el bueno* (a good) person to know because I was connected.

I said, "*Pasame la receta compa...*" or something like that; figuratively, it means "share the wealth, homie."

We exchanged handshakes and I told him I'd hit him up later on his cell number.

Another street theater performance down, Tony Awards, here we come.

After a few days and spending some time with our analysts attempting to get an identification of Flaco... I finally called him.

"Oye mi Flaco, es el Gallero. You plugged in?"

We agreed to meet in the parking lot of the same shopping center. An operational plan was completed, and the team was briefed. In all undercover operations, an op plan must be written and disseminated to the troops so that we all work off the same script.

Surveillance units were given their assignment. The note taker was tasked to monitor and write down the activities. Rescue units were assigned to cover us. The supervisor was in place to monitor our conversations. A few other roles are best not written down right here. The intended purpose of the op plan was to keep everyone on the same page. We did not deviate from the op plan;

with this supervisor, there was only plan A. Not a plan B. We didn't like it, but he was in charge.

Flaco was a real squirrelly kind of crook, very street smart. A predator like him had to be to survive in his world, where dog eats dog. A longtime client could turn and be his next attacker, or even worse, the next guy he met could be someone like me.

Our surveillance units arrived and set up earlier than usual. They took their assigned vantage positions covering entry and exit routes and us. Like hunters stalking their prey, we waited.

Surveillance reported that Flaco arrived several minutes early. He took a position in the very middle of the busy grocery store parking lot, wolflike, scanning the area for other wolves and prey. He was being careful to blend in so that the protectors of the flock, the sheepdogs, wouldn't sniff him out. Meanwhile, around him, families hurriedly parked their cars minding their own business. Mothers placed their children in car seats like herds of harmless kind-hearted sheep. A few walked into the grocery store, others into the pizza restaurant. Husbands urgently walked into the store with their list of groceries written on a piece of paper mamma had sent them with after a day's work. Amongst all of that, we were about to meet Flaco the Mara Salvatrucha, most commonly known as MS13.

We were the Sheepdogs he looked for—his worst nightmare. Many men like him never saw us coming. We were nearly impossible to detect because we wore the faces, had fangs, projected violence, and the swagger of a wolf. We also were very familiar with the risks we were taking... the chances of losing our lives or even ourselves for a hundred, a couple hundred thousand dollars, or a million worth of marijuana, cocaine, methamphetamine, or heroin.

We did it anyway.

In our hearts and minds, it was a higher calling we answered. Others considered us as risk takers. They were absolutely right. Being a Police Officer, Special Agent, or Investigator isn't enough for some, so we operate undercover, associating ourselves with some of the evil people living amongst us and exposing ourselves to risks only known to those like us. Much like a soldier, sailor, airman, or marine who aspires to serve in a more specialized way than they already do, it's the same with the undercover operative.

Our colleagues treated us slightly differently, commenting and even doubting our integrity.

"How can *you* afford a car like that?"

Occasionally we'd get stopped for "going too fast," where we then got a little extra attention. Our command often paid particular attention to our ways and means, requiring us to subject ourselves to additional random drug testing to keep us honest, so they said.

I swear the laboratory staff must have thought we were some recently released dangerous hombres as often as we were there to drop.

We trained for just about every scenario. We wore no body armor, no uniforms, or badges. We relied on each other, our training, our handguns, our wits, and a pair of gigantic balls. We ensured our vehicles were clean and the registrations matched our stories.

Undercover work was not for everyone. You screw up, you get shot in the face. It quickly separated the so-called rockstars from the '*oh, I'll do surveillance* guys.' It was dangerous work, and our job was to go into dangerous places.

Andres and I intentionally arrived a few minutes late. We hadn't agreed to an exact spot with Flaco. We pulled in and drove around the lot once. I called him and told him to meet me on the east end of the lot against a block wall.

A good undercover does their best to control the drug deal whenever possible. If this seemingly casual meeting suddenly were to *break badly.* We at least had a backstop if rounds went off. Aside from that, we owed it to our community to keep them safe. The last thing you wanted was an innocent child or somebody's grandmother getting caught between the big bad wolf and a sheepdog battling for supremacy. It was always better to meet in places where the chances of an innocent civilian being exposed to danger were limited. Even with preparation, sometimes you can only partially predict what could go wrong or where the threat may come from.

My mind went to the day Don and I were coming back from a meeting with a prosecutor at a non-disclosed location when we remembered we had unfinished 'relationship building' in the area to do. Acting on a tip, we drove to a trailer park occupied by Mexican Nationals. The park housed mostly laborers looking to work, raise their families, and mind their own business.

As we pulled in, the fresh *carne asada and beans* being grilled wafted through our windows. Everywhere we looked, trucks with ladders, scaffolding equipment, and orange water jugs in the back had parked where we parked. We could hear dogs barking and see kids wearing spider-man backpacks walking home from school.

Everything seemed normal. It reminded me of how I grew up. Amongst the typical day-to-day living and the construction worker trucks was a trailer we suspected was occupied by some players. We weren't sure if they were big-time players or small-time players. In places like that, we would never know.

I've gone into trailer parks and been inside homes where military-grade duffle bags loaded with cash were guarded in the back by some indigenous-looking Mexican nationals.

It was our job to go into places like that and find out.

Don told me he would monitor me from our car, a sick ass mustang 5.0. I would walk up and ask for *Primo. It* means cousin but is commonly used by Mexican nationals to describe a buddy. Our only intel was that one or two players would be there. We had met them before in a meeting with other traffickers. If for some reason, Don was no longer able to monitor me, he'd give me a quick 'hurry the fuck-up' honk, and we'd be out.

Simple, easy we got this.

We parked and I got out. I intentionally rolled down my window, then shut my door and knocked.

A male voice in Spanish asked, *"quien chingados es?"* Who the hell is it?

I replied, *"El chino, está el primo?"*

It was enough to let me in.

The male was in his late twenties or early thirties. He wasn't dressed like the construction laborers in the neighborhood. This man wore designer jeans and handmade leather sandals like tourists buy in Mexico. He was dripping in gold jewelry and wore a spotless dress shirt.

I wasn't sure if I had met him before.

My mind drifted to the many scenes in the HBO series *Sopranos* where they sit and seemingly talk about nothing, but you know they're talking about something. That was us for three minutes.

He seemed comfortable talking to me.

I spoke to him as if I had met him once before.

He stood and said, *"esperame tantito,"* held up a finger to indicate that I needed to wait for a minute then went into the back of the trailer for what seemed seconds. He comes back out into the living room.

I stand up.

He walks towards the kitchen, peeks out the side window, pauses at the front trailer door, and locks the bottom lock of the doorknob.

I had seen dopers do that before. I never liked it. It wasn't a good sign. It made me nervous.

Something had changed.

I walk towards the door.

The man turned to face me and asked me what I wanted with them, *"Que quieres con nosotros."*

I don't recall if I gave him an answer because I was fixated on the hallway where his other buddy was now standing. He was wearing a white wife-beater, or as my pal and fellow undercover brother and Author Lou Valoze calls it, *an Italian smoking jacket*, holding a chrome-plated Smith and Wesson .357 revolver in his right hand.

If Don were going to come in and rescue me, it would have helped if the door had been unlocked.

I had to get out. As I stepped close to the door, I felt a hand, and then an arm came past me from behind on my left and onto the door.

Immediately, he locked the deadbolt installed just above eye-level with his right hand.

How could I have missed that? I turned and had to think of a plan fast. I had to deliberate fast but also be very smart and methodical. At that very moment, elements of my life flashed before my eyes like a slideshow. From right to left, I saw a kindergarten photo of my son, then a flash of a photo of me when I was about the same age as he appeared in the picture. Although I acted confused with this guy who was now less than arm's length away and his buddy still at the entry to the hallway, I was also formulating a plan in my head.

I politely asked him to let me out and apologized for any inconvenience.

He didn't respond.

The guy in the hallway pointed the gun toward the carpet to a huge dark brown stain.

I had noticed it before but having seen so much other crap on carpets in this line of work, I assumed it was an oil stain. This one wasn't. I looked at it carefully as if my binocular vision suddenly had zoom capabilities. It was blood. *How did I miss that? Jay Dobyns* is right. Undercover *work is a vomit-covered scab.*

The guy says to me, "*Eso eres tu*," meaning that's me right there.

I again asked my guy to let me out, but a bit more aggressive this time.

He refused.

In a matter of seconds, I formulated a plan. If I asked him a third time and they still refused, I would grab the guy right in front of me and shoot him in the head. I would then use him for cover then shoot the other man. It all played out in my head, my body reacting to it, and my adrenal glands had dumped enough adrenalin it was convinced I was doing it.

Time slowed down for me.

Then suddenly, the guy with the gun said, "*Bajadores le hicieron eso a mi compa,*" jackers did that to my friend. He looks back at me with his revolver still in his hand and his other hand and forearm up against the wall.

Just as I was about to ask them to let me out for the third and final time, he told the guy in front of me, "*Sacalo a la chingada,*" get him the hell out of here.

The top deadbolt came open, and the bottom one, too. And I got out.

Physiologically I was still in the fight.

I got into the car.

Don looks at me and says, "What the fuck took so long? I was about to honk! I couldn't hear shit."

I'll paraphrase what Vincent Cefalu, author, and retired undercover agent, once wrote: "*Just because a gun is taken out in a drug deal doesn't mean they're gonna use it. It is a drug deal, after all.*"

A passing car in front of me snapped me out of my reminiscing.

We saw that Flaco was looking right at us.

Being heads-up crooks ourselves, we had backed into the block wall in case we had to run from jackers or cops. We were in my undercover gunmetal gray Firebird. I was driving and

Andres was taking shotgun. Andres was good at playing the part of acting hard yet indifferent. He was leaning back in his seat with his cell phone to his ear as if he were busy talking to some chick, his eyes always on me and our target.

Flaco rolls up, his engine left running, the car facing the wall, and gets out quickly. His time was money, after all.

Because we had difficulty identifying him, we implemented methods to get close-up imagery of him and his face. This guy looked like the serial killer Richard Ramirez, the Night Stalker, except Flaco had a shaved head.

We talked at the driver's side of my car. I opened my door and stood towards my car's rear fender in case my partner had to take a clean shot.

Flaco's demeanor showed that he was in a hurry. He got close and personal. He asked what I was looking for, *"Cuantas chivas quieres aquí tengo?"* He showed me what he had on hand. Chivas was slang for heroin, and he wanted to know how much he wanted.

I turned it down. I wanted pounds, no, kilos of that shit.

We knew what he was capable of, and I clearly was no junkie. We agreed to meet another time.

He bounced.

Surveillance reported that he drove like a bat outta hell, leaving the parking lot. The team was able to land him at a local apartment complex, but because none of them fit in, they weren't able to identify where he lived.

What a rush it was, looking at a killer in the eyes. Walking away from a drug deal was a rush too. Saying no to what he offered wasn't easy. If he suspected us as cops, he didn't anymore. Cops would never *just say no to drugs*. Right?

Flaco called me the next day, but we had decided to make

him wait another day, besides our intelligence unit was still working on getting a good I.D. on him. Even with facial recognition, we had some challenges.

In the meantime, I received a call from my source.

The CI said he had gotten wind of a guy, an old acquaintance from Mexico, who was connected in town. The guy was looking to get rid of a couple of keys of cocaine. He described him as a real player, dangerous and missing a few fingers on his right hand.

According to my confidential source, they had been cut off by *mafiosos* in the southern region of Sonora, Mexico. The source said his hand looked like a *pinsa de langosta*, a lobster claw. Had his fingers been cut because he stole something, or did he owe people money? We didn't know, but we would soon get to know Langosta.

First, we had unfinished business with Flaco. An operational briefing was prepared by me and approved by my supervisor. We were going to meet Flaco. The plan was to get as much dope as possible, put him away, and hopefully send him back where he came from.

I briefed the team and handed the op sheet to everyone. Assignments were made, and routes were covered. A SWAT team was there, not the County one I had mentioned before, nonetheless, these guys were squared away too, effective. They had covered me multiple times on several buy-bust ops, high-risk undercover meets. I trusted them with my life every single time. I knew from previous experiences that this team didn't take well to undercovers making tactical suggestions.

Some teams are open to it and take it for what it's worth, just advice, and sometimes act upon it if it makes sense. These guys, well, they were too cool, it rubbed them the wrong way. Too much ego. With that in mind, I offered a suggestion regarding taking Flaco into custody safely. I suggested they deploy straight on us and exit from both sliding doors in a half-moon shape instead of a single file formation. The idea was to contain Flaco between my vehicle, his, the unmarked SWAT vehicle, and the wall. I didn't get much of a response, just a half-assed smirk and a slight head nod from the team leader. Who was I, after all, to suggest such highly trained tactical Spartans?

Because I knew Flaco was squirrelly, his head was always on a swivel. I suspected he was either going to shoot it out or run. It's hard even for the coolest SWAT dude to run down a determined bad guy high on adrenaline while wearing an additional 40-50 pounds of gear on your body.

The briefing was completed, and the advance surveillance team reported they had located Flaco leaving his apartment complex. They followed him carefully to see if he stopped elsewhere to pick up the goods. He drove straight to our meeting location, arriving about ten minutes early.

The exact location as last time.

Flaco was extremely cautious. He parked his car in the middle of the busy parking lot, walked away from it, and walked towards the grocery store entrance, while looking around and into the parking lot.

We pulled in and went straight to the eastern block wall. We backed in doing our own threat assessment. I called Flaco.

He said he'd be right there and hung up the phone.

As expected, he pulls up in the same manner near our car, nose in; the car engine is left on.

Perfect.

Except for this time, he had in his hand a pound of black-tar heroin wrapped in plastic.

I took a few seconds to look at it, ensuring surveillance had enough time to get a grip on what was transpiring in this thing we call Street Theater. I did my best to keep him facing east.

SWAT boys were coming from the west.

SWAT made their move.

I made my move and tossed the dope toward Andres, making it seem like I was going for my money.

Flaco was extremely nervous.

So was I, but for different reasons than his.

One of the most dangerous moments in the life of an undercover agent is when both money and drugs are within proximity of each other. Anything can happen, the undercover can be ripped off or, worse, killed. Once the police are introduced into the picture, no one knows how a suspect will respond to the possibility of losing his freedom.

Would he go shooting it out with SWAT? With me? Fight, give up, or run?

It is why we trained so much. We called them 'what-if' scenarios.

In moments like these, cool heads must prevail, and sound tactical decisions must be made under pressure. By preparing for the worst, we expected the best outcome.

As SWAT pulled up, they intended to park their vehicle fully perpendicular to ours. But I'm sure for good reason, they stopped short and, per their plan, kept it facing north. SWAT deployed from the side door facing us in a single file or a stick formation.

Flaco was gone.

I didn't have to jump for cover inside my car.

Flaco was no longer a threat to me. He ran fast and north as if his life and freedom depended on it; he scaled the 6' or 7' block wall 50 yards from our vehicles like an Olympic gold medalist.

The closest SWAT guys to catch up to Flaco were the driver and the team leader; both gave chase. Neither caught him. The look on that team leader's face as he huffed and puffed back was priceless.

To maintain our covers, Andres and I were taken into custody by uniformed police and transported away.

We got arrested a lot.

My undercover vehicle and the evidence were transported to "Mary," code for our HIDTA office.

In the meantime, all hell broke loose in the immediate area where Flaco was last seen. Uniformed patrol units quickly responded to the site and deployed small unit tactics to search for him. An air unit responded as well.

I got a hold of a patrol radio and began monitoring the situation.

911 calls started coming in, and it was broadcast that a male matching the description was seen jumping fences and running through yards.

I thought, "Maybe we can catch him after all."

A call came in; an elderly woman had been assaulted and taken into her home by a man possibly using a gun.

It was him. He had seen her arrive with grocery bags, and since it was now getting dark, he forced a helpless woman into her home.

By the time it was reported, first to her daughter, who reported it to the police, several minutes had passed.

He was gone.

A second call came in like the first. A man said someone broke into his backyard and then into his home. Police responded to the area but were a little late.

A third call came in like the first two, and nothing. K9 units deployed in the area, as well.

It was too late now, and no other sightings were reported.

We lost him.

The following day we had a post-operational briefing, which is standard. Most of the law enforcement units involved, along with a few SWAT officers, attended. It seemed no one took personal responsibility.

I told my boss that maybe had I done more by getting him

closer to the back of my left fender and closer to the wall… perhaps we could've contained him.

Our supervisor agreed but didn't like it.

I also voiced my opinion and stated had SWAT done a better job at cutting him off with a half-moon shape deployment…then maybe Flaco's avenues of escape would've been limited.

My supervisor and the SWAT supervisor didn't like my and Andres' analysis. My supervisor had been a longtime member of that team at some point in time and had close relationships with them.

SWAT took it personally, too.

Post-operational briefings provide feedback and look for ways to improve and learn from our mistakes. Unfortunately, in some organizations, one guy's victories are often seen as shortcomings or losses for the others who didn't win instead of seeing it as an opportunity to improve.

As far as I can recall, the case became a robbery-assault case, and *if* Flaco was ever found, a drug sale charge was to be added.

Police work isn't an exact science, we practice it and sometimes we make mistakes. -Kevin Grogan, US Army Veteran, Author & former Narcotics Detective.

ACT 6
DIRTY JOB

Operation Langosta was set.

I spoke to him on the phone, and we agreed to sit and talk. I told him I was looking to purchase a few *carros blancos (*white cars-- code for cocaine) from his lot, and I needed them to be reliable.

We agreed to meet at a local Baja-style restaurant, but only after I held an operational briefing of course with the team. This was a very high-risk meet because, unbeknownst to Langosta, we prepared to mind blow him with cash to draw those keys out.

I wanted to see what he was made of, and if he couldn't come through, he and I would never work together again. That was my message to him over the phone. That message was made clear again when we sat down to chat.

Langosta showed up on time.

Andres was with me. Although he spoke little Spanish, he

knew enough and was legit enough to vouch for us as drug dealers. We had requested County SWAT to cover us in the parking lot for what was to happen, except our boss requested his boys, the same guys who had recently lost Flaco. We needed three or four for cover or rescue.

Langosta and I got to know each other a bit during the meeting. It was the usual stuff like where you are from, the weather, baseball, and dopers like to name-drop to boast their worthiness. I acted unimpressed with whom he was acquainted but took mental notes. I maintained a 'get to the point' demeanor because I had shit to do. Like in sales, the one who talks first or the most typically loses, and he wouldn't stop talking.

The ruse was for Andres to take a call before we completed negotiations. I would ask Andres to take the call outside. Like a good soldier, he stood, didn't acknowledge our man, and went into the parking lot.

Langosta paused for a moment and stared at Andres as he walked away.

I wondered what was going through that criminal mind of his. Maybe he was hoping he'd never have to deal with him. If you know what I mean, my primo Andres could turn on the charm.

We finished our beer, told him I would be waiting for his call tonight, and wanted ten white cars. He said he could put together half tonight.

Fine.

Show time, stage left, and Andres was the star. I dropped two twenty-dollar bills to cover the beer and chips.

Langosta and I walked toward the exit.

As we stepped onto the parking lot, Andres was in his undercover car, supposedly stopping near the exit to pick me up.

Instead, Andres stopped in front of us with the passenger door nearest us. Just as planned, the tinted passenger window rolls down.

I motioned to Langosta, and there, in its glory, was the pot of gold at the end of Langosta's cocaine-covered rainbow.

We flashed him $100,000.00 crisp dollars fresh out of the HIDTA safe.

He wasn't expecting to see this; he swallowed hard and paused.

Now there was no doubt in his criminal mind we were serious. I tapped on the car's roof like an ambulance, and just like that Langosta's rainbow was gone. I turned to Langosta and told him he would not see that paper again, to put to rest any plans of ripping us off until he brought us our kilos of cocaine. I left in my Firebird making sure nobody was following me.

Drug dealing is a dirty business, deceitful. Mike Rowe should do an episode on *Dirty Jobs* to feature the filth, the dirty schemes, the backstabbing, dead baby carcasses stuffed with heroin, the hangings, the senseless murders, and the broken families associated with this job.

It was August 2005, approximately noon, it was hot, and we had some planning to do for my final act.

We briefed our supervisor who was wanting to get a feel for Langosta.

Can he come through with all the coke, is he trying to sniff out money or cops? Did we observe any counter surveillance inside the Baja bar and grill?

Our surveillance units had him locked down in a house in a nearby track home-style neighborhood. We did not have enough to hit the home yet. We didn't have the facts or circumstances to substantiate a warrant either.

Everything checked out, and I decided to meet Langosta for a second and final time. Our form of street theater was performed to appear improvised and organic. Our preoperational work was premeditated and intentional. We planned for everything possible that could go wrong. We often trained for it by simulating worst-case scenarios with one another. A doper can show up with the coke. We count it. He gets arrested. Doper shows up with friends in the same car and brings the coke, we have to make sure we have enough manpower for that. Doper(s) show up and think we're easy targets and try to rip us off. We've got that covered. Dope dealer doesn't come through and are no-shows, move on, it happens. What could possibly go wrong? A larger contingency of SWAT Officers was put on alert.

Within two hours or less, Langosta called me and told me he found the cars I was looking for and could bring them to me today.

I told him I'd call him back, and I could hear the disappointment in his voice. I wondered what he was thinking, but I had to put him off. For one, I needed more time before agreeing on a time to meet and location, and I didn't want to seem eager.

Complacency and being overly eager can get you hurt in this line of work. Too many undercover operatives have been killed by suspects who later admitted the reason they killed the cop was either because the agent was too lax or too naïve and eager. Agents have been killed by suspects who didn't know the victim was an undercover operative. You never know where the danger may come from.

Because of the nature of this bad guy, the amount of the anticipated cocaine transaction with a potential street value of over $100,000.00, we covered all of our bases. This particular time we had a fixed-wing aircraft on standby to help with surveillance, ground uniform units within blocks away, and a cover team.

SWAT was split into two teams: an arrest/rescue tasked to take everyone into custody, me included. The other team acted as a secondary arrest team/containment.

By this time, I had already called Langosta back and told him I was good for it but was running an errand for my old lady, and I'd have to call back to lock down a time.

My supervisor started the briefing by describing the suspect and our intelligence on him. Our ground units informed us where he would be coming from, making it easier for surveillance units to track his whereabouts.

Did I forget to tell you the name of my supervisor?

Amongst the team, we called him "Naw'n Stuff" because he

said that a lot, and he wasn't open to suggestion much. Don't get me wrong, we called him that name, not to his face, of course, amongst us as a way to deal with his leadership style. Up to this point in my life, I have been exposed to many leaders and have seen various leadership styles. Because of my work, most supervisors were very black-or-white in their decision-making since we worked in the gray. They sometimes would not consider the complexity of our undercover work. I'm sure having to be right all the time was hard work.

Cops are comfortable amongst what is familiar. Most are led through managing or directing people on what to do. Few supervisors took the time to get to know their subordinates; if they did, it was because they had something in common.

I was a good follower and had learned the right time to ask questions and when not to. I'm not saying all law enforcement or military leadership is the same. I was aware of and have met legendary leaders in both. Truth is that law enforcement officers want to be led rather than managed.

It is possible that "Naw N'Stuff" intended to do his very best, but his personal distractions may have kept him from it. It's probably why he spent so much time with "Beth," the prosecutor. Did he think we weren't going to notice? We were trained observers, after all. I have to give it up to Donnie "Don" Bertch. Some people have that natural ability to lead when the boss couldn't or wouldn't. If it weren't for Don stepping up as often as he did and being able to make suggestions to "Naw N'Stuff" to get him to be open to our operational suggestions, some cases would not have been completed.

In his book, *5 Levels of Leadership,* John Maxwell describes the leadership levels.

A level 1 leader holds a leadership position by rank or title. People follow him because they must.

A level 2 leader is followed by people who've given them permission by relationship. They want to follow him.

A level 3 leader produces and brings results to the table.

A level 4 leader is now producing duplicate leaders just like him and is followed because of what the leader has done for the team.

A level 5 leader is the pinnacle of leadership. This leader is producing leaders who produce leaders just like her and most of it is based on values and principles.

JOHN MAXWELL

I recommend all Maxwell books.

We respected "Naw'n Stuff" as a level 1 leader and nothing else. At least that's where he stood with us.

"Naw'n Stuff" made his assignments. He was detailed. He was reading off the op sheet I had handwritten to include the location of the meet and verbal arrest signal he had suggested and I had approved. Without giving too much information or disclosing too many details, the SWAT arrest team was clear of the arrest signal.

Once the arrest signal was given, I was to lay slowly onto the asphalt parking lot like I had done a hundred times before, and SWAT was to take Langosta and me into custody. Andres was to walk away and be picked up by "Naw'n Stuff."

The briefing was turned over to me. I stood in the front of the briefing room, looking at the same guys who had lost Flaco. I provided what little history I had regarding this suspect. I reported I had not seen any weapons on him, nor had the topic of guns come up. I described his clothing as of a few hours ago from my last undercover meeting with him and the vehicle he drove. I also went into detail about his missing amputated fingers.

I reminded them that my co-case agent and I would be wearing the clothes we were in. I was in a red untucked patterned oversized button-down short-sleeved shirt, light blue baggy denim shorts below the knees, white low-top kicks, and white no-show socks. Andres had his hair in cornrows, an oversized blue polo shirt, and dark oversized jeans. We were both always armed. If an undercover was to change their clothing after a briefing, the team needed to be aware of it. It's an absolute 'no-no,' and I'm sure it was added to the op sheet because at some point the ball was dropped by an undercover cop. **Don't change the Op plan.**

Once we had covered the op details, everyone got ready to

go. Surveillance officers double-checked their fuel, radios, and backup batteries. The note taker prepped his forms, "Naw'n Stuff," our tech, aka: "Gadget," and I checked the audio equipment. The pilots walked to the hangar, looking very cool, I might add. Meanwhile, SWAT put on their body armor over their woodland BDU-type camouflage uniforms. Their thigh-holstered .40 cal Glocks were double-checked, locked, and loaded—earpieces in, helmets on, and their M4s on 3-point slings at a low ready.

What could possibly go wrong? If it did, we had it covered.

I made the final call to my bandit and settled on meeting in an hour and a half. Our units still had an eye on him at the house he had landed at; he had not moved. A contingent of the team arrived early at the location, including the SWAT arrest team.

Langosta didn't know it yet, but the meeting location was the same as last. It worked for the area.

He agreed to the meeting.

The rest of the units remained close by.

Andres and I got into my undercover car; he drove. Here is where things started to slowly fall apart. As we approached the Baja restaurant I mentally started checking operational items on my list and learned we still had the bag full of money. Why didn't "Naw'n Stuff" secure it? He signed for it. We called him, and he told us to stash it in the car. It wasn't what we were supposed to do. Since we weren't intending on walking any money, I couldn't risk our bad guy seeing it again.

Could I have canceled the op and told the bandit it would have to be another day? I didn't.

Instead, I reached back and tossed it over and behind the back seat and into the trunk/hatch of the Firebird.

Upon arriving, Andres received a call from his wife informing him his father had been in a near-fatal car accident, was in critical condition, and doctors weren't sure if his father was going to survive.

Langosta was now ten minutes away, and dusk was on our western horizon. Because it was getting dark and harder to see, the SWAT Team Leader, the same one huffing and puffing behind Flaco, decided to make a last-minute change to the arrest signal. He said they were having tech issues because it was about to be dark. Surprisingly even "Naw'n Stuff" approved that change. He wanted me to lift the hatch to my car. I suppose I could have refused. After all, he was deviating from the op plan. I didn't because I felt it was a good call under these conditions, and I still trusted them to cover me.

Our bad guy, Langosta, arrived quickly and pulled right next to us, facing west along my passenger side whereI was seated. Andres and I had gotten temporarily distracted talking about his dad's current situation.

SWAT requested we park at the end spot closest to the raised median of a parking lot in the middle facing west. There were no cars in front of us. With a straight shot at us, SWAT was located to the north 200 feet away.

I exited my car on the passenger side, Andres on the driver's side, and stood there like he'd been instructed. I asked Langosta about *my things*, and he said he didn't have them. His eyes glassy and a bit crazed; he chuckled and asked for *los papeles,* the paper; the money.

I was angry and wanted to lay his ass out. Was he attempting to rip us off? Was he trying to flex like we did earlier today by showing him cash?

A car races into the lot, a white dodge sedan with two big 'ol Mexican nationals, *paisas* as we called them. They got out of their vehicle that was parked facing west about five spaces north away from mine within reach of SWAT.

I remember them wearing white pants; dress shirts, and one had a ball cap just resting on the top of his head.

Langosta says, "they have 'em." Grinning from ear to ear like *El Guapo* from the film *The Three Amigos*.

In the drug business, few times do deals go as planned by either side. I had to be flexible. It's street theater, after all, and we had to be able-bodied thinking actors in this improv scenario. The doper brought friends who showed up in their own car.

No biggie, where do dangerous men go? You got it—dangerous places.

I proceeded to walk to the car of the *paisas*.

Andres stayed put on overwatch, keeping an eye on me leaning over the roof of the Firebird looking in my direction. He was a Marine, on the County SWAT Team. We had been in several live fire training scenarios dozens of times, and several real-time drug deals together.

I felt confident. Where would the danger come from? Why was Langosta looking so eager, confident, and not the usual nervousness I'd seen before in people? *Does he think I have the money on me? Did they plan to separate Andres from me?*

I needed to make sure I wasn't in the line of fire. Then one of them opens the trunk and says something to me in Spanish *alli estan*; they're right there. I started counting the cocaine kilos, again slowly.

SWAT wasn't moving.

Time slowed; seconds tick-tocked like an eternity.

I remembered, "That's right, SWAT wanted the hatch to my car open." So, I walked to it, but the dopers were now asking for their money. It wasn't supposed to go this far. An arrest should've already been made.

Andres should be long gone, and I should already be in custody.

Nothing is happening.

I get to my car, and Langosta looks concerned. I am purposely stalling because I'm hoping SWAT or someone copied my transmission and told SWAT to move in.

Nothing.

Everyone was waiting for me to open my hatch, including the three bad guys around and behind me. But the money was in there, and I was not about to give it to them. Evidently, SWAT was waiting, too.

Andres was always faithful, watching closely. We make eye contact.

Langosta got suspicious after he asked me again for the money as I was opening the hatch, but noticed my hesitation, it was locked. *Keys?* Wait, Andres drove. He has them. I was out of excuses. It was either, I put up the cash or we were going to have problems real fast.

I opened the hatch; I acted as if I couldn't reach it. I play stupid and look to my right and see SWAT moving. My back is entirely towards them. Apparently, Langosta did too.

Once SWAT deployed, I did as instructed and per the Operational plan, I stepped away from the vehicle with my hands up and slowly. I lay on the toasty black asphalt beside my closed driver's side door between the parking median island and my car.

As I lay down, I saw from my right peripheral vision that Langosta had gotten into his car and sped off like NASCAR driving right over the bushes in front of his car and the raised concrete elongated parking median. The parking block created a loud bang, and flashes of sparks flew.

The situation was getting worse. No one was in a position to chase or stop Langosta and the parking lot was getting busy with people enjoying the evenings with their families.

As I lay face down in the parking lot I saw that Andres had walked backward and gotten into the passenger side of our supervisor's vehicle. Just as planned.

There are so many real-time worst-case scenarios an Undercover Drug Agent can train for. What happened next turned out to be the catalyst for the next chapter in my life.

At the time, I didn't see it that way, and it sure as hell didn't feel like it.

Between the sounds of multiple flash bangs and the moans of grown men being taken down hard to my left and one near my left foot right next to me, one was moaning louder than the other due to a flash bang exploding between his legs.

Amidst all, I made out the sounds of a SWAT Officer, my rescue, and my backup coming in to get me. The cadence of their familiar footsteps is unforgettable. From experience, I knew that any second, I would be pulled out of harm's way. Having unsecured and possibly armed suspects near you and under those conditions wasn't safe. It was a very high-stress dynamic situation; they always were.

Instead of being pulled from harm, the SWAT Officer trotted up to me, took a stuttering step, then kicked me under the chin as if he wanted to put my head through the uprights. I saw the boot coming and couldn't believe my eyes. I felt the impact on my head and face causing my body to be pushed toward my car. In confusion, I blacked out but wasn't sure and that wasn't it. He kicked me again near my ear and jaw and stomped the back of my head, left arm, and elbow. He chose to stand on my elbow/forearm and grind my arm into the parking lot asphalt.

I was confused, fighting to shake off the cobwebs in my head from the kicks and the shock of it all. Blood rushed out of my nose and mouth. I could taste it. I could also taste and feel the rocks from the dirty parking lot inside my mouth. I wanted to talk, but my mouth wouldn't respond to the words I was forcing to come out. I wanted the ground to swallow me. I was in fear for my life. This cop was going to shoot me if he noticed my weapon in my front waistband. I always carried my Glock 19; I trusted that 9mm with my life, but it was useless to me right now, and this wasn't something we trained for. If I fought, I was disadvantaged in more ways than one. So, I tried to bring my arms in to cover myself, but he applied more pressure. I still couldn't talk.

My lower jaw was protruding out past my right ear, it seemed.

All I remember him saying was, "If you did what I told you to do, this wouldn't be happening to you…if you did what I told you to do, this wouldn't be happening to you…If you did what you were told to do, this wouldn't be happening to you."

His words did not sound like police commands to me.

A small part of me sensed as if I was being punished. *Was it just a daily dose of street justice that occurs on this side of town to guys like me, or did I have it coming?*

I tried looking up to my left, where he stood, but I couldn't see his face. I noticed he would look around, scan, and repeat his threats while changing his foot from my elbow to the back of my head and neck area. *Was he saying those things, so his SWAT buddies heard or acknowledged him, he had to know it was me. Right?*

This level of force continued until they had handcuffed the other two suspects, taken them into custody, and secured the scene. I could hear one of the other SWAT Officers tasked with handcuffing or flex cuffing bad guys speaking to them in broken cop -Spanish.

That confirmed to me he recognized they were the suspects, when he finally made it my way, I noticed he was speaking to me in English. He for sure knew it was me. He had to.

I was overcome with a sense of relief right away. He flex-cuffed me.

He applied the cuffs very lightly, not in the same manner you would cuff a suspect whom you suspect would try and get away or be a threat.

By now I had been cuffed a hundred or so times before.

He stood me up.

I became very agitated and semi-combative. Head injuries make people respond in unpredictable ways. It was a state of confusion for me, anger, and embarrassment.

As the SWAT Officer was handling me, I tried to pull away and he instinctively held me back and told me to calm down. I clearly remember telling him *to calm the fuck down. At* least, that's what I meant to say. I'm not sure what came out of my mouth. I took a moment to gather my wits and asked the SWAT cop to look at me, "Look at me! Turn me around."

He did, and when he did, he looked confused and asked me who did this.

I looked behind him, motioned with my head, and said, "Him" as best I could. You never know where the danger is going to come from. I would never have guessed it would have come from the most senior SWAT guy on the team.

I had respected this man; he was older, experienced, and wiser. He had covered me numerous times and knew exactly who I was. I trusted him on multiple occasions to protect my life in tight quarters, from hotel rooms where I had to meet a notoriously violent cocaine dealer to nighttime vehicle takedowns where I was seated right next to the suspect with weapons pointed at him. I wanted him on point if he was on one of my Ops.

The SWAT Officer holding me sat me onto a curb towards the front and to the north side of my vehicle. The SWAT operator who assaulted me, let us call it what it was, an ass beating, who I'll name "Operator," stared at me with no expression. They then walked away.

Blood kept coming from my mouth and nose, and the pain in my face, jaw, and ear was bad.

It was nighttime now.

I looked around and noticed my supervisor's undercover vehicle passed by me inside the parking lot.

Andres was in the passenger seat. The look on his face said it all. What happened? Did the bad guys jump me?

People came out of the restaurant, and a few stopped to stare.

Shamefully, I looked away at the ground. I was sitting on a bunch of tiny ants, which had crawled all over me. I didn't care. My gun was still tucked in my front waistband. So many thoughts were going through my head... my mother and kids. I don't even think my kids knew what their father did for a living. They joked a lot that I reminded them of the dad from the animated series *American Dad*, an animated sitcom about a dad who was a secret agent.

Maybe they did know something after all. In their tiny hearts, however, I was their superman.

I was still flex-cuffed behind my back, which was probably good. I saw the secondary SWAT team leader looking at me from a distance with no real expression. We went way back; we knew each other.

Out of earshot, I saw the SWAT team tasked to cover me get into a huddle. It was an 'oh shit' huddle. They looked at me a few times. I couldn't read their faces, and they wouldn't look me straight in the eyes. To be quite fair, there were two who came to check on me separately, the huff'n puff'n team leader from before, who asked me if I was "ok."

I don't even know what I said back then, but I remember thinking, "What the fuck, man?" Maybe I said it.

He left.

The other one was concerned. He apologized and asked who had done this.

I told him, and he left looking concerned but more confused.

I waited for my supervisor, "Naw'n stuff."

He never came to me. I'm sure he had a good reason. I waited, continued to sit, and watched these guys pull their heads out of their asses. I kept waiting for medical attention. I figured at any moment; I'd hear an ambulance pull in.

Nothing.

I was being treated like a piece of evidence. Don't touch it, don't go near it.

Finally, it was a uniformed police officer who had responded to provide scene security, and as he walked up to me, I told him I needed medical attention.

ACT 7
A VERY THIN BLUE LINE

Law enforcement regularly face three traumatic experiences for every six months of service.

SCIENCEDAILY.COM

I love the good men and women who represent the Thin-Blue Line. I want to protect them. Because of the brotherhood I was committed to, it took me years for me to share my incident with outsiders.

It hurts my heart to have to write and tell this story.

The field is full of great men and women who want to serve, to do good, be a role model, ninety-eight percent are great cops, incredible fathers, and exemplary husbands. Law enforcement can be a thankless job most of the time, everyone criticizes what we do, even boring at times, often repetitive yet filled with moments of sheer terrifying horror.

Imagine that over a ten or twenty year career.

The ambulance finally arrived, the same guys who I teased and called second responders, but have much respect for, took good care of me.

At first, they weren't sure why I was sitting alone, still handcuffed with a gun protruding from my shirt.

I told him I was a cop. *Really, I was... I was one of them, but was I?*

Another police officer came by and secured my weapon and cut one cuff loose.

Upon arriving at the hospital, so many thoughts came through my mind. Part of me was a little embarrassed, too. I didn't want anyone who I might recognize to see me and know I had gotten beaten like that. I was told my wife was on her way, it was 8 or 9 PM and I figured the kids would be asleep and our nanny would stay with them.

Internal affair types showed up, looked at me but didn't say anything to me. Not one of them asked how I was feeling.

It was a busy night in that emergency room and there were no rooms available. I was left laying on a gurney in a hallway. The only person upon arriving at the hospital up to this point who showed any form of empathy or compassion was the janitor. He asked me if I was ok, in his own words he said, "Looks like they fucked you up bro... Hope you're ok," motioning to the uniformed officers who had been requested to secure the hospital ER upon my arrival.

Since I was still wearing the flex cuffs on one hand, he assumed I was someone who had been arrested and beaten up by police. He was right. Sort of.

There were so many moving parts to this situation, agencies, and locations that I purposely have not and will not name out of respect to the good men and women still or now in them. They shouldn't pay for the wrong doings of their predecessor's and their leadership. Another investigation that went bad. I never learned the outcome and what transpired with the one-hundred thousand dollars, the cocaine, or whatever happened to Langosta.

Medical staff began to treat me, they treated me extra nicely once they figured out that I was an undercover cop, but they still couldn't find me a room.

Because of my head and face injuries, I was scanned for internal hemorrhaging. The white in my eyes was now red on both sides, my face was swollen, my head throbbed, my jaw felt like nails were being driven in between it and my ear. I was bleeding from my nose, I was bleeding from my mouth, chin, and left cheek, I had fluid coming from my left ear. I had boot marks on my left elbow, the side of my head, and the back of my neck. I was demoralized.

I never expected to get beat up like that, especially not from cops.

Thoughts of my mother and dad came into my head. I excused myself to the bathroom where I vomited from as a result of the head trauma and the stress of it all. I stared in the mirror and said, "How do I explain this to my kids?" I got emotional and my eyes teared up. I just couldn't help it. I cried without making a sound as the nurse and doctor examined me.

"It's ok." The nurse said it was normal for eyes to water or be emotional after head trauma.

That wasn't the only reason why I was crying.

My wife showed up. I wasn't told that she had arrived. I happened to see her standing there just watching me.

She didn't say a word initially.

I found out later she thought from the looks of things I had been shot in the face.

Years later that moment came back to haunt me and I came to the realization she didn't say a word while she stared at me on that gurney. Nothing. I always assumed when a cop is sent to the hospital, a wife who thinks it's a worst-case scenario, like a shot to the face, would make some sound, a gasp, a cry, tears, and emotion. I got nothing.

She stood there until I asked her to come closer to me.

Doctors informed me that the police were wanting to speak to me. I was well aware who it was but wanted nothing to do with law enforcement bureaucrats. Since I knew they were closely listening in, I asked for privacy and was given the opportunity to lay down in the chapel towing my IV bag, wearing my hospital gown. I had kept my shorts on so my ass wouldn't hang out.

I was informed they were looking for a bed to admit me for observation, but it could take a while due to the patient load.

My sister, Judy, came to see me and I love her for that. After the bleeding had stopped, the pain subsided with the delivery of some good intravenous narcotics. I was cleaned up and I had to allow the police to take photos of me. I was in fact evidence now, so it felt. Because the doctors couldn't find a room quickly, I chose to leave against their recommendations. I wanted to be near my children and get away from all of these cops.

The ride home was quiet, like a kid who had gotten in trouble at school.

When I entered the house, Gabby, our nanny, quickly came to me. When she saw me, she cried like a mother who'd seen her son get hurt.

The children were asleep.

I took my bloodied clothes off and took a shower.

From that moment, my life completely changed, my friends changed, and my world became different. *Have you ever been so focused on life and where you were going that something comes along and changes everything?*

Unbeknownst to me, but I was at a crossroad and had to tread carefully.

A few days later, two Internal Affairs Detectives from the SWAT agency that assaulted me came to my home to "allegedly" interview me and take my statement. It was part of their investigation since I had filed an excessive use of force complaint, this visit was not a surprise.

In-fact, they interrogated me for nearly four hours.

The interview was cordial enough to begin with but changed quickly once they started asking pointed questions regarding my actions on that day.

They asked.

I answered.

They asked again differently.

I answered the same response as before.

Repeat.

Their focus of the internal affairs investigation was regarding my actions at the scene of the take down, not the "Operator's."

The more I attempted to explain his actions, the more they asked about mine.

"Well, did you try to identify yourself?"

"It's hard to do so when your mouth is falling off."

"Why didn't you badge him, were you being combative?"

"Why, why, why?"

"Were you acting like a suspect, were you using foul language?"

This interrogation… I mean… interview went on and on. So long, in fact, that I had to ask for breaks and excuse myself to take my pain medication. The fact that didn't sit well with me was that they were investigating their own under such unique circumstances.

ACT 7

Let me jump ahead a bit here, a jaw specialist informed me my mandible had been permanently damaged, the ligaments had been overly stretched, damaged beyond repair, and would require lengthy therapy. I would have been better off had the "Operator" just broken my jaw he said, at least that they could have repaired. The bleeding in my eyes would stop once the pressure wore down. My left eardrum was damaged and today sounds at a certain decibel create vibrations inside my ear.

A neurologist declared me unfit for duty because I had sustained a traumatic brain injury (TBI) which explained the headaches, tinnitus in my ears, chronic vertigo and the nystagmus in both eyes which lasted almost daily for four years.

The traumatic brain injury left me susceptible to more permanent damage and I was told I could never expose myself to that chance again, at least not for several more years. I had become a liability to a profession I loved and the men I worked with on the team. It was suggested that I medically retire after months of rehabilitation.

I went through a lawsuit, which I lost four years later because I couldn't get the opposition to tell the truth and I had accepted worker's compensation for my treatment.

As I read the "Operators" deposition, I learned it took all of forty-five minutes of the Internal Affairs investigators time.

I discovered the investigation was all about what I may have done wrong. "How was he moving? What was Pimber saying? Did Pimber act like a suspect?"

I've been asked if any sort of disciplinary action was taken against the "Operator" or the team. In short, he was written up for failing to identify an undercover law enforcement officer. The SWAT team received training as to where on the body to apply force on a suspect, specifically, not to kick a suspect on the back of the head or face unless it involves a deadly force encounter.

That's it.

My lawyer was right, if we win great, if we lose it's tragic, but he did warn me of the following. He warned win or lose, once I cross that thin blue line, I would never be welcomed back. It was a chance I was willing to take because I couldn't just sit there and do absolutely nothing. I had to fight back the only lawful way I knew how.

"Operator" was later promoted to a supervisory role and as fate would have it, he was terminated from the team and demoted for reporting drunk to a SWAT call.

The worst part of it all was that I had lied to my children. Unlike my father, I lacked the courage to tell my Nicolle and MarcAnthony their *American Dad* had been beaten up by the police. For years I let them believe I had been in a car accident.

Post injury and several times throughout my case I received threatening calls from cops on the SWAT team.

Andres did as well. It was always, "Hey rookie keep your mouth shut."

Not to mention the random encounter I had on the street.

Something, I later learned and found profoundly interesting and unbelievable at the same time was the fact "Naw'n Stuff" claimed there wasn't a clearly audible enough body-wire recording of the Langosta buy-bust and therefore he couldn't provide one. I provided one, all two-and-a-half minutes of me getting my ass beat. It didn't matter.

I was left with many unresolved and unanswered questions like the call I had received from Tio Pancho shortly after my assault. Tio Pancho, at that time, was on another assignment and far removed from where I was at the time. He called me and told me in Spanish, "Supe que la traian contigo, pero aquí no puedo hablar…te hablo" *I heard they had it out for you, but I can't talk right now… I'll call you later.*

I never did get that second call. Tio Pancho never called me, he died ten days later.

After the lawsuit I even received a bill from the opposition's legal team for approximately $650.00 to cover photocopier expenses they incurred. Unbelievable.

They added insult to a broken and already badly injured person.

ACT 8
MEN WITH NO FACES

When you have a TBI, you're usually the last one to learn.

Between whispers everyone else seems to know something is not right with you. Initially I had chronic tinnitus, headaches, daily vertigo, and chronic pain.

I noticed I felt like a dull pencil, no longer sharp; I was fading.

There were a few times I experienced my vision become distorted, my horizon no longer horizontal, my brain didn't register it that way. My neurologist referred me to a few specialists, and one happened to be for speech therapy. No, not because I couldn't speak, but because I was having trouble tracking words from left to right. A brain sensitivity/tolerance test was administered.

I was so embarrassed and within a few minutes I froze.

The test was simple, I thought. Listen to a recording where a person reads numbers to you, two single digit numbers then you add them and say the total out loud, take the total and add the next number the speaker provides you. Easy, until the pace picked up.

Here's an example *2, 3 "=5", 3 "=8", 4 "=12"* it went on for a bit. Then, it got a little faster. Then, a lot faster. Before I could recognize it, I had frozen. I was catatonic. My eyes were wide open with tears streaming down my face. My mouth was open and my eyes were shifting left to right. The exercise had triggered nystagmus.

I became angry at the therapist for not warning me this would happen. I don't know how long I was out. After the appointment was over, I sat out in my truck for an hour or two because my head was badly shaken. I called my wife, but she didn't answer so I drove home. I was driving when I shouldn't have been. I slept a lot too and spent many hours alone at home. My perception of reality started to change.

Because I was no longer working undercover and suppressing the memories of the near hits and misses with activity, everything came to a crash. Like a train on its tracks that suddenly stops, and everything comes crashing forward.

My once busy days were replaced with empty space and my mind filled with fleeting thoughts of hopelessness and helplessness. An idle mind is indeed the devil's workshop.

I was taking multiple pain killers, oxycodone, hydrocodone and chasing them with a twelve or a twenty-four pack of beer a day. Valium for my chronic vertigo, Neurontin for my restless leg syndrome. If I was drunk enough early, I'd fall asleep mid-day on the floor with my feet on the sofa and wake up that way at 10pm to discover everyone was already asleep then either stay up all night or take some meds to help me sleep. Repeat.

I was trapped in a vicious cycle.

I was a total mess.

I was breaking badly.

Then the nightmares came and for several years I had the same recurring dream. Men dressed as soldiers in full tactical gear stalking then chasing me. I was either being chased or watching them chase me. Sometimes, I would be running with them, and suddenly, they'd turn around and come after me. I would have nightmares of men without faces holding me down and injecting me with heroin. I dreamt of shootings except my weapon would malfunction.

My nightmares would include me just walking and a man would turn the corner and shoot me in the face. I could see the flash of the gun barrel explode. I would often wake at night in a sweat from dreams of fights I had been in, except now, I was losing in them.

The nightmare of soldiers chasing me happened with such frequency I would drink myself to sleep with hopes that I wouldn't have them. My nightmares woke my kids sometimes.

My wife would complain I would kick and punch so much in my sleep that she was concerned for her safety. I was so worried these so-called soldiers in my nightmares were coming to get me that in my drugged and drunken state, I would visualize how they would enter my home.

I became paranoid and I imagined they would enter my home using a dynamic entry method. They would breach my glass door using explosives; it played like it was on loop in my head. I kept my gun nearby and adjusted my bed, so I could have some tactical advantage. I even rehearsed it because I accepted it in my mind to be real.

I was breaking, but I didn't know it yet.

I had a medication schedule and a drinking schedule to go with it. Not one Doctor showed any concern for my chronic pain-killer use… I was a cop, remember? They trusted me. I had stacks of pill bottles. I was a drug dealer all over again. My head wasn't right. I would drive and get lost. If I watched a movie with my daughter, I would cry over the slightest emotional Disney scene.

I was falling apart. But I couldn't tell anyone.

My speech therapist recommended I read books to help with tracking and brain tolerance. My moods became unpredictable. I was short tempered. My kids avoided me, my wife avoided me, no one called me. I kept taking the pills and chasing them with Miller lights. I stopped for a while but kept drinking and hanging out in places where I used to meet bad guys. Then, the ideation of getting even and suicide crept into my mind, and it wouldn't go away.

I became obsessed with suicidal thoughts and obsessed with the details of where "Operator" lived. I had very bad intentions for him. I also became very familiar with the whereabouts of his wife who was also a cop. I'll just leave it at that. Those two obsessions fueled my anger.

Suicide was at the forefront of my mind. I would picture the how, the where. All of the time. Post-Traumatic Stress is a devil, it robs you like a thief. It happens not because you're weak, but because we are noble men and women and not born with the predispositions to do evil or harm onto others yet in facing evil we experience these events as protectors. We have to understand we can only take so many *I'm going to die moments* in our lifetime. It's like the lid on a jar, sometimes it starts to leak and that's a sign that the jar is too full. It's time to start emptying it because you can only avoid the triggers and reminders for so long. If you do nothing it will make its way into your heart and it will eventually break you.

PTSD, it's like the devil is in the room with you. - Victor Avila, Ret. HSI Special Agent, Author Agent Under Fire

One night I recall being in a lot of pain, I was also being treated for depression during this time. Because of the pain I was experiencing I decided to take pain medication and had taken valium to control the effects of my vertigo. I drank way past my limit and without any warning I started visualizing my suicide, every detail, even the funeral.

I stumbled into my bedroom, wearing the clothes I had on for three days, then sat on my bed in the dark contemplating it. My gun even spoke to me telling me to do it, "Come on… do it."

Suddenly, there was a change in the air within the room. A horrible smell floated through the room. A scent I could only attribute to the devil. I smelled evil in my room. I could actually feel something was in the room with me that had brought such a foul odor. The closest thing I can describe that stink is death. I had seen plenty of dead bodies in the desert, been to the morgue more than once, and I knew what many slowly rotting corpses smelled like together.

It scared me. I started crying, not out loud, it sounded more like an angry moan. I found myself crying for my soul. I had just enough wits to put blankets over my head and forced myself to sleep. I learned at that moment, what some of my colleagues who had been down that fatal tunnel may have experienced before making such a final decision.

The LAPD Behavioral Sciences Service reported that death by suicide in law enforcement is 1.5 times more likely to occur than on duty deaths. These being some of the leading causes:
- *Alcohol and/or Drug Abuse*
- *Administrative/ Legal Problems*
- *Depression*
- *Financial Problems*

- *Exposure to Trauma/ Adverse Life Events*
- *Negative Self-Image*
- *Physical Illness/ Retirement/ Chronic Pain*
- *Family History of Suicide/Violence/ Abuse*

I was slowly beginning to check those boxes.

My wife meanwhile watched TV in the living room, my daughter and my son slept quietly in their rooms. Their superman, their daddy was at death's door.

I woke up the next day giving thanks to my Lord for my life. I was thankful to be alive to fight another day. At that very moment, I got up, grabbed my Glock 19, disassembled it, and we parted ways. I once trusted that gun to protect my life under very dangerous circumstances but was now threatening to take it. I did not touch it again for at least two years.

With a clearer mind, I came to realize I was beginning to crave the medication, the euphoric recall I was experiencing with the chronic use of pain medication started taking priority and was constantly in the forefront of my day-to-day thinking. I came to terms I was going down a path and into the arms of a giant bigger than I could ever battle.

I weighed the consequences of continuing to use the medication being prescribed to me in good faith, by good Doctors, or doing without them. I choose pain over the possibility of addiction and the chance of slowly losing my soul. I stopped the meds and dealt or rather managed the pain and the ideation of suicide through cross-fit exercise. To this day, I run twelve to sixteen miles a week and have competed in a few 5ks, 10ks...I even managed to take 1st place in one.

Running has helped me to remember I can push past quitting on myself and it is an excellent opportunity to reflect. I had to become an active participant in my own rescue, sought counseling, and kept kindergarten pictures of my children close to me to help me remember I had more to live for. Their image deflected evil.

I also consulted *Dr. Kevin Gilmartin, PhD*. He and his associates of mental health therapists are regarded as the tip of the spear in police psychology.

Over the course of numerous painful sessions, I was put in a position to have to talk, which I found difficult to do. It's not easy to tell on yourself. It was one of the first times I noticed my inability to remember certain things and found my introspective thought process would bring me to a hard pause. In turn, causing me to lose my train of thought, not because I couldn't remember, but because I would find myself going back and reliving events. If it was not for the counseling, I wouldn't have remembered. The more times we met to talk the more comfortable I became. I learned how to intellectualize my situation; to process it differently and use language that didn't trigger my heart but would trigger my brain.

I had to use words such as, *it was an unfortunate event that happened in my life, but I'm ok now* to describe my incident. I practiced that mantra during my runs for a while. Sometimes, I still do.

I learned to accept I was mourning the loss of my career and that it was ok to mourn, although I denied that I would. I was told I was going to miss it. Boy did I ever. I missed the camaraderie. I missed the danger. I missed my partner Andres, Vincent T, Tio Pancho, I even missed Don.

I mourned being that *guy,* the undercover narc.

I missed the streets which provided us the stage for the street theater we performed in. I missed the cleverness of how we got the job done and the adrenalin that came with committing crimes in the name of the law. I missed having a mission all under the color of our authority.

I was suffering through an identity crisis. I felt as if I had once been a sword wielding Samurai who had now been condemned by his master to becoming *just* a gardener. But I also understood *it was far better to be a Warrior in a garden than a gardener in a war*.

Most importantly, I learned although I would never forget the betrayal, the violation of the presumptive trust that existed among the man who turned on me, or the rumors that had been started about me. I had to forgive all of it.

I had to come to terms that my mental health was more important than my career.

I reached a point through my counseling session that I had to accept someone did something they should not have done and that some people testified to things they didn't actually see. It was difficult to hear men from that same team, *my team*, make statements based on hearsay about me. Their intentional half-truths misled investigators and harmed me. It took a lot for me to come to terms of having to forgive, because part of me wanted revenge.

I had it, after all, all planned out.

I carried that burden, plot, the anger in my head and it made my heart heavy for several years. Until one day four years later.

I said it out loud as I was advised by my counselor, "I forgive you…I forgive you."

I had to, it was eating me inside and I was losing.

A hostile and destructive force had clearly instructed me to kill myself, but God spoke to my heart. Because of that, I gave forgiveness a shot.

I was glad I had reached that level of clarity because three months later I found myself shopping at a chain store with my son, MarcAnthony, on the opposite side of town from where I lived and I didn't normally frequent. While we stood at a register, I was overcome with a sense of awareness and compelled to look to my left, then behind me, and there he was…

"Operator" was standing behind me.

I turned and noticed that he had a nervous off-guard expression on his face. I looked at him as if he were invisible because I had forgiven him. He no longer rented space in my head. As we walked into the parking lot, my son asked me if I knew him, I said, "No, son. I thought it was someone I knew…"

It's important to note by that time in my life, I had started carrying my concealed sidearm again. The respect between my gun and myself had improved.

We had reached an understanding.

I know exactly what I would've done had my heart not been in the right place. Sadly, I would have gone away and become known for one bad act instead of the many good ones in my past and what my life was to become.

ACT 9
WE CREATE OUR OWN LUCK

Unknown to me yet, my path to reinvention had begun the day I laid bleeding on that dirty, hot asphalt parking lot.

My growth began when my speech therapist recommended, I pick up books to help my eyes and train my brain to track from left to right. I read numerous books: *Donald Trump*, *Robert Kiyosaki*, *Jim Rohn, John Maxwell,* and numerous others on personal development. I also re-read *The Art of War by* Sun Tzu.

From Trump, I learned I too could create a legacy with my incredible children and make a name for myself.

Kiyosaki helped me visualize my future goals. I had to see things with my mind and not so much with my eyes, vision.

Sun Tzu reminded me to appear strong when weak, the art of deception.

Jim Rohn helped me comprehend that with proper preparation and timing, I could create my own luck.

John Maxwell reminded me you get one shot, because life is not a dress rehearsal.

My reinvention journey started shortly after I asked if I could volunteer for a year for a local developer, Mr. Tom Bailey. I'm grateful for his mentorship. I was given the opportunity to observe how a small subdivision was built. He allowed me to show at 6AM and observe all day long till the last contractor left. Because of his mentorship, I was able to implement the vision taught to me by Kiyosaki. I was able to build my own new construction rental duplexes in the area where I grew up as a child. I built new houses on the small empty lots where I used to pretend to play army, cowboys and Indians or cops and robbers as a child. My newly found vision allowed me to build several brand-new rentals, even demolishing the home where, as a child, I lived in the garage with my family. I replaced it with a brand new three-bedroom duplex that I rented to families who qualified for section-8 housing.

Remember the Police Officer who broke my dad's ankle?

I was invited to become a member of their city council board on standards and codes for their employees where he once worked, in the same town where I was building my homes. I was invited into the same municipal building where the Police Sergeant had taken my father's statement.

I learned at some point throughout this five year struggle my wife had been secretly dating a member of the SWAT team which had assaulted me.

That fact kicked my ass.

After numerous challenges, a market crash, and bankruptcy, I divorced her.

Jim Rohn helped me bring preparation and timing together (preparation + timing = luck) and see the opportunity in it. In Jim Rohn's famous words, "Here's how it happened for me."

I was visiting new friends one evening when his wife told me she was working as an extra on a film. The director was filming for a Mexican network, Cablevision. She asked, "Weren't you a soldier or a cop?"

I replied, "Yes, both."

She then told me the director of the film needed someone who was proficient and experienced on how to handle weapons and who could instruct his actors, but the person needed to speak fluent Spanish.

"That's me!" I blurted.

I realized I had just gotten lucky! Jim Rohn was right. So many times, people forget their fortune, good or bad, is sometimes based on their timing, preparation, and their attitude.

If the timing presents itself but you're not prepared, you're out of luck. I so happened to have spent years preparing, the time came, and I got lucky.

The director liked me. He started showing me the rehearsal footage of me instructing the Mexican Actors how to handle a weapon and clear rooms. He said I looked good on film and invited me to 'read.' I didn't know it then, but it meant to read some lines, to audition.

All I knew was to be myself and he liked it enough to write a part for me in his dramatic film, *Sexo en Paraiso*. Upon completion of the film, I found acting became therapeutic for me. Cathartic. Acting had allowed me to relive similar moments recreated on film in a safe environment where I was certain no one wanted to kill me.

It was street theater except it was all caught on film. There was a call-sheet like our op sheet where assignments were given, complete with a cast of characters each with their respective areas of responsibilities. A script and a supporting cast whose job was to capture our performances and record them. Gadget guys who would equip us with listening and audio devices to capture what we said. The difference was, we were given multiple takes and opportunities to get it right and people liked us.

With the support and guidance of a fellow veteran turned film writer I was encouraged to share stories of my undercover work which were subsequently turned into a screenplay by another writer. Those stories were shot and packaged into an award-winning dramatic short film I co-directed and starred in, titled *DURESS*.

In this film, I featured and recreated the brave and ethical men who I had worked with, the men who chose to face head-on the wolves who preyed on our communities and turned innocent children into misguided youths. The honest and not so honest Americans that were turned into drug users and addicts; into people who would trade the love of their children for their next fix and exchange their morals and ethics for a drug profit.

I play the drug dealer in the film, the bad guy.

There is something about playing bad guys I found so liberating.

You can find *DURESS* on my Youtube.com/LouPimber featuring Andrew McClaren and Elliot Ruiz both United States Marines now turned actors who had fought in one of the bloodiest engagements, The Battle of Fallujah.

I challenge you to find a more realistic film or TV series than what you will see in *DURESS*. The film sparked a real interest in others and in me to become a professional actor, and after showing it to a talent agent, I was signed. I found an acting coach and eventually landed a recurring role in AMC's award-winning series, *BREAKING BAD*.

Now here's where preparation and timing led me to.

During the filming of one of the scenes, I was asked to climb onto the side of a *Pollos Hermanos Truck*, seemingly out of nowhere a jib mounted camera pans right up to my face and holds. This scene was considered a stunt by industry standards. In that very moment, in my mind, I went to my sixth grade water fountain memory and recognized I had accomplished my goal of *stunt man. Was it a mere coincidence? I don't think so.*

No one knew what I was experiencing at that moment, and I wasn't about to tell anyone, nor would *Walter White* or *Gus* care.

Life has a way of taking your goals and dreams, turning them into reality and sometimes bringing the past into the present.

During filming, I noticed that the last name of a lead actress was the same last name "Judge" had. I had to know. So, I asked her if she was related to him. It was her father. She was the oldest daughter who had already moved out of the home and onto college to pursue acting by the time I had begun my investigation.

I told her my name.

She immediately acknowledged it from the police reports. It's when I learned her father, "Judge" died shortly after leaving prison.

In an earlier chapter, I wrote how the TV show *WISEGUY* inspired me to work undercover. Preparation and timing also put you in places to shake the hands of people who have inspired you. You see, during one of our *BREAKING BAD* filming days, I found myself in a passenger van on our way to a location shoot with Aaron Paul who played "Jesse Pinkman," Giancarlo Esposito who played "Gus," and Jonathan Banks "Det. Mike".

I had the privilege to tell Jonathan how he and Ken Wahl had inspired me to work undercover and briefly told him my story. To make the current goosebump situation even better, he took his phone and called Ken Wahl to tell him briefly about me and to wish him a happy birthday.

I had a wonderful time on set, unfortunately many of our scenes did not make the final cuts, but no one can take away that experience for me. On a side note, I almost did not show for the audition. I had heard too many already well known actors had been turned away.

If you expect to win, half the battle is often having the courage to show up and be counted on.

I discovered a real opportunity to continue my path of reinvention. I found the best form of revenge was to put myself on a path for success. I played the lead role in numerous television commercials like Audi, Credit Unions, waste management, electric companies, and played a Spanish speaking dentist for a local kid's dental commercial. I've appeared on numerous billboards, my face appears on the sides of buses for a national advertiser, various other national print ads and several printed commercial advertisements with both of my children. I also volunteered and supported film students from the local university.

Acting taught me humility because I wasn't always the best fit for the part. It taught me to play on a different team and different people and it revived my creativity. I spent time at The Fox Studios meeting with and advising Brian Grazer's writers from his TV series *GANG RELATED*. Writers like Benjamin 'Ben' Lobato *QUEEN OF THE SOUTH*.

I was lucky enough to have appeared in an episode (preparation *timing= luck)* and worked with RZA, providing him with some pointers on how to clear a room with a weapon and make it look realistic. I also was able to tell him how WU-TANG had been the musical track to my days working undercover in a gang unit. I was given the opportunity to act in the *EWTN Network* film, *KATERI,* A film commissioned by the Vatican. I performed utilizing the Mohawk language for a leading role. As I write, the film *RUSTY* where I appear in a co-starring role, can be ordered on Amazon. Acting allowed me to reconnect with retired undercover agent and New York Times Best Selling Author, Jay Dobyns, *NO ANGEL*. Jay Dobyns is one of the most creative cops I've had the pleasure to work with and get to know.

I was honored to be asked to play a leading character in his short film *BIG RED FRIDAY, the* story of a retiring undercover operative and the dangers associated with the work. This film has been viewed thousands of times by lawmen worldwide and received raving reviews.

ACT 10
POST-TRAUMATIC, SUCCESS-DEVELOPMENT

Reinvention is a tricky thing, like success, it requires payment upfront. You have to do the hard work first, make the sacrifices before you see any changes in yourself. It takes a person to be honest with oneself upfront, to admit fault upfront, to take personal responsibility for one's shortcomings and allow room for improvement; be open to criticism.

No matter how good we may believe ourselves to be, we aren't, and we are not as bad either. At least most of us fall somewhere in between. At some point in my law enforcement career, I had been told we could only be good at one thing. If you are a great soldier, a heroic cop, a high performing entrepreneur it's likely you're not the best father or husband, it works the other way too.

Where you place your full attention is where you will likely excel. I'm sure there are exceptions to this theory. I admit that throughout my law enforcement career I caught passing glimpses of this theory in action. Some people are better at spreading goodness around. Taking this concept into consideration, I decided to look back and work on my shortcomings.

I chose to start where my heart was and that was with my children. I was certain they had inadvertently seen me at low points in my life and I did my best to be a good example. I made it a point they would see me reading on a regular basis if I was going to ask them to become leaders. John Maxwell taught me leaders are in fact readers and there isn't a problem that hasn't ever been written about.

They too picked up the good habit and it provided me the opportunity to give them books on personal development for young readers. We had direct conversations on what they had learned from their readings and conversations on their future plans and goals. I helped them understand not everyone is going to be just like them. Therefore I wanted them to see those people as ones they can help lead or learn from.

I stressed the importance of being ok with making mistakes along the way. My daughter competed in gymnastics and my son in little league baseball. They became each other's biggest supporters and their hardest critics. I stressed they have respect for one another and respect for their peers. I wanted them to become stressors of society so long as the pressure they brought on was for a positive reason. It was my way of inoculating them against the negative influences and choices to come. I made it a point they understood I was their father first, their friend second, because of it, disagreements will come and yet it was all going to be ok.

I stressed they learn to be in the moment and appreciate it although they are looking forward to the future.

Attention to detail was a topic I often brought up and emphasized. I encouraged them to associate themselves with people that have similar levels of ambition and expectations, but also to choose people ahead of them in life because it doesn't make sense to be the smartest person in the group. To level-up.

I was facing an inward battle. I understood everything began with me, and I needed the courage to change. For generations, military leaders have described courage as, *not the absence of fear, it's facing what you fear in spite of it*. John Maxwell went one step further and described it as, "having the power to let go of the familiar and forge ahead into new territory."

I had to let go of what was familiar too, I had to step into unknown territories, part ways with a few people who once had influence in my life. I had to be open to forge new associations. As someone who had lived a life of service with most of it in law enforcement and in a covert environment, I struggled with letting go of what was familiar. I struggled with being in a group of people where I had little to no control of. I had developed an unhealthy hyper-vigilance, but because I understood I would always have to be aware of my surroundings. Over the years, I managed to adapt it to being situationally aware.

I also developed a new level of appreciation for the RODs I

had worked with. I appreciated that their years of service had developed unique skill sets only ones who had been around for some time could appreciate.

I was focused on being the best undercover narc, that meant, that I had not been as focused on being the best version I could be as a father. I was willing to trade time spent with my children with more time spent with crack dealers, marijuana, cocaine, methamphetamine, and heroin smugglers. I had closer relationships and fulfilling conversations with certain members of my team than I did with my family.

I had spent my life writing and chasing goals but somewhere along the way I missed that growth was important too. I was planning detailed elements of my career before having made a blueprint for my own life. I was backwards.

I thought I was growing; but I wasn't.

I was learning new things, picking up new skills and abilities. I was improving, by accident, not intentionally. James Allen wrote in *As a Man Thinketh,* "People are anxious to improve their circumstances but aren't as willing to improve themselves."

That, as it turned out, was me.

My assignments and my duties improved, but I wasn't improving personally, from the inside. Sadly, that very unfortunate event in my life forced me to understand this and because I came to terms and accepted it as just *an unfortunate event in my life,* I was able to make changes.

I came to terms with the post-traumatic stress which had been consuming me for so long until one day when I was given the opportunity to hear Clinical Psychologist, Jordan Peterson, Author of *12 Rules for Life,* share as long you are clear in your heart and conscience and have a definite understanding between right and wrong, I would be ok.

Those words spoken to my soul. I didn't allow it to become a *disorder* for me.

Instead of allowing it to continue as a post-traumatic stressful event I used it to become an opportunity for post-traumatic stress development.

I learned I had to experience and *live* through a low point in my life so that I could be able to see and honestly appreciate my current and improved situation. There was a silver lining in all of it, after all, because I discovered there was life beyond law enforcement.

You probably have noticed there are a lot of I's in this book. I do reference myself a lot, it's because everything had to start with me. I had to take full accountability and next spent time further developing those soft-skills I wrote about earlier. I fully understood that the hard skills got me employed and selected into special assignments and do 'cool-guy' stuff. I later learned both through observation and reading post my injuries that it was the soft skills that lead you to growth. I learned to sharpen my communication. It's a work in progress for me to be able to speak in a positive tone. I am slowly becoming better at persuading others by understanding what mattered to them. I had to understand and learn to appreciate my worth, but also to make sure I brought value to the people around me whenever possible.

In the world I came from, it was common to hear people gossip about one another and the ills of the world. Therefore, I had to learn to process these things differently. I had to learn to intentionally speak well of others.

It was my emotional intelligence that I comprehended needed a lot of work. The world of law enforcement is filled with emotion and despite that, cops don't have or make the time to process these emotions; ever. Because of it, we often have experienced moments of rage or respond with aggression when dealing with issues because this is typically how we solve problems in the field. We normally fixed things quickly through force or violence because there was no time for emotion. These coping mechanisms or lack thereof tend to make their way into our personal lives as well and are often the root cause to the leading issues resulting in workplace conflict, disciplinary action, firings, divorce, and suicide.

In 2016, I remarried.

I married a beautiful independent businesswoman, Rhonda. A leader in her own right, a Realtor with twenty-two years of experience, former Vice President of Marketing for a national builder, and a mother of two talented beautiful young ladies, Ashley and Stephani Verhalen. Together with them, through her modeling agency and magazine publishing they mentored the youth and young women of our community.

With awe I observed Rhonda Moretti bring a community together like I had never seen anyone before, her motto was

Building Beautiful Confidence, and it was that confidence and dedication that attracted me to her.

Rhonda Pimber's legacy will be forever seen in her *Bellezza Models* students who because of her compassion for them will forever see the best version of themselves. I never quite understood why she didn't come with me to the *Breaking Bad* finale cast member party in Hollywood shortly after I first met her. You might want to ask her. I'd be curious to hear what she tells you.

In that same year, we pursued entrepreneurship on a national level. We found a need to be part of the fastest growing insurance and financial services marketing company in the nation. We were actively recruited to open a market in our state and address an epidemic of financial illiteracy that has been spreading throughout the nation. We've mentored and trained several hundred agents, some of which are now senior brokers running their own offices. Our business has expanded into multiple states. We are always actively seeking ambitious overlooked people to be a part of our national crusade; Rhonda's strategic planning has been the driving force behind the leadership development in our business and her encouragement helped me write this book I'd been putting off for the last few years. Keep an eye out for her book to come.

Entrepreneurship has changed my life. I've learned to lead people, not just manage them, to lead with moral authority. I've learned to carefully balance how to challenge and encourage people along the way. I have had the honor to be mentored by

Great American Entrepreneurs like Chris and Mary Philp who united they're saving America, from whom I've learned that whenever adversity comes and shows its ugly face to see it as *an awesome* opportunity.

Of course, every time an emotional challenge comes, I have to *take it a step back* because after all it's probably *good for me*. Overall, I've learned that Crusaders *Die Hard*. I've become friends with fellow entrepreneurs Javier and Annel Castro, Javier a twenty-one-year military veteran, five years in the United States Marines and sixteen in the United States Army 10th Mountain Division and have had the pleasure to mentor couples like *The Mouth of The South,* Andrea & Antonio McGowan, and of course the beautiful families like Oscar and Alisha Lopez.

The Entrepreneur himself, founder of PHP Agency Inc. and host of *Valuetainment*, Mr. Patrick Bet-David imparted in me if I plan on, and in order to do something big in my life, I have to be prepared to make new enemies, new critics, deal with the rumors of what I'm doing now. I will need to learn to solve bigger problems because it is far better to be wise than smart. I've had some incredible times with Patrick Bet-David, the Philp and Castro family and because of our relationship we've been able to venture off to faraway lands to both vacation and hold business meetings that have helped me develop as an entrepreneur.

Along the way I've had the distinct honor of personally meeting people who once were only known to me on paper. I had the pleasure of personally meeting Mr. Jordan Peterson and had the great fortune to hang out and socialize with Mr. Robert

Kiyosaki at Patrick's home in Florida. I recently had the honor to spend time with Author Mr. John C. Maxwell and tell him how much he helped me along the way. We shot a short video where he delivered a short thank you message to my law enforcement brothers and is looking forward to reading my book. Somebody pinch me.

My mother would always tell me, *"Dime con quien andas y te diré quien eres…" tell me who you are associating with and I'll tell you who you are.*

She was absolutely right.

I've attributed the Post Traumatic Success I've had to three things, the people I have associated with, the books I have read and the meetings we often find ourselves being a part of across the United States and in various parts of the world.

In 2021, my wife and I capitalized on an opportunity to expand and now reside in Texas. To be quite honest, I needed a change of scenery. I needed new places that wouldn't remind me of my past life and experiences. So far it has been helpful and has expanded my vision a bit. I have no doubt sooner rather than later I'll fulfill my dream of having a ranch with a horse or two and of course a pack of German Shepherd dogs, my very own noble protectors; sheepdogs.

Entrepreneurship has given me the opportunity to dream again, rather, it has forced me to dream like I did when I was a child writing my goals on pieces of paper. For too many years, I had stopped dreaming, visualizing myself winning and being on top. I was existing, going through the motions.

I'm learning to live on purpose now.

Over the last few years, I have had the opportunity to be booked to speak to numerous police organizations, companies, and groups across the United States on the topic of post-traumatic stress, entrepreneurship, reinvention of self and the American Dream.

So far, my children have grown to become productive Americans. My daughter Nicolle Pimber-Coy is in the medical field currently serving in the Air Force and on deployment to Qatar, her next goal is to pursue becoming a Physician Assistant upon her return. Nicolle probably doesn't know but as a child, in her own way and with those pretty little brown eyes, she held me accountable. I couldn't let her down. She is married now to a Great American and US Air Force Veteran, Landon Coy. She was inspired to serve upon seeing her little brother MarcAnthony complete his US Army Basic Training and Military Police School at Ft. Leonard Wood, Missouri in February of 2019 as an enlisted Soldier.

I will always remember the day I got a call from him during week three into his training. His voice cracked as he thanked me for the hard lessons that I had taught him growing up. I'm sure highly motivated drill sergeants were making him move with a purpose and that may have 'inspired' him to call me and tell me, "Dad, thank you, you were right."

MarcAnthony is now in his last year of college. He was awarded an ROTC Scholarship and will be commissioned as a 2nd Lieutenant in the Spring of 2023.

Being a single parent came with its opportunities to answer their questions and address the challenges in our lives together. I am so proud of their growth and development. To this day, I keep those kindergarten pictures visible near the visor in my truck because you just never know where the danger comes from.

To my law enforcement brothers and sisters, life after retirement can come with its very own set of challenges. One of the hardest things for me was finding what to do with my time and dealing with the loss of my identity. For most men and women who have served their country or community, their whole identity was of a warrior or lawman and it is ok to miss elements of it; it's going to happen. You're still the same person, your mission has changed, if you allow it.

I found it both difficult and helpful to speak to a counselor and process issues. Lack of an identity and purpose are some of the causes of excess drinking, depressed moods, and suicide. If you find yourself in a tough situation or know someone who is, call *1-800-COPLINE.*

I had the honor to interview Charles Stringham Ret. LA County Sheriff's Dept., training coordinator for Copline. That interview titled, *When Cops Need 911, They Call the COPLINE* is posted on my YouTube channel. COPLINE listeners, as they are called, are all retired law enforcement officers who have been expertly trained to hear you out, help the caller to find solutions and offer vetted resources.

To my brothers in blue,

You're a cop at heart, your service doesn't stop at retirement, you still have the skill set and the mental clarity to see what the average person does not, but you have no authority other than the nobility in your heart to serve and protect others; you'll always be a protector you're just going to do it in a different way. If you pursue other work, I recommend you choose a field different from law enforcement because it will allow you to make new friends and different associations. Perhaps in future writings I can describe to you what I did to move with a purpose and achieve personal growth as a parent, husband, and entrepreneur.

I recommend using your retirement to spend time with the family that stayed close to you and let those who weren't close, know you love them, and you're there if they need you. Read a few good books. I've listed a few here, they will teach you a different language to speak which will help you attract new friends. No matter how your career comes to an end, don't get back to the same type of work right away because it's familiar. You're either not ready yet or you're not giving yourself a chance to grow and get away from that gruff, negative way of processing issues and often talking you either were a part of or near to for so long.

ACT 10

I stayed away from anything law enforcement related for many years for the reasons I mentioned. A few years later, I did establish a great working relationship with an organization providing high level personal security and close protection work for clients and have deployed a time or two to places both inside and outside of the US and safely travel with or covertly bring back Americans who found themselves in harm's way.

I will always be a protector.

I wrote earlier in life we don't always get what we want, but we get what we deserve... arguably there may be some truth to that I suppose. I'd also add we get what we set our focus and our thoughts on when things outside of our control happen to us.

You'll get what you really deserve when you learn to stop using your challenges and unfortunate circumstances as excuses.

I'm in a constant battle with myself and when I'm down, I remind myself I will always be that trained soldier, an above average law enforcement officer, mediocre actor, and an up-and-coming entrepreneur. I don't regret any of the experiences I've shared with you. I've learned to accept it was a privilege to have lived with them.

If you're reading this and think, I have it together. Stop now. There's a reason why I'm writing this book; it's for me as much as it might be for you or someone you know. I experienced so many emotions doing it, had trouble sleeping, the words kept running through my head on loop.

I'm thankful for the many opportunities and challenges that have come my way, there's a special place in my heart for the bad ones. I still have trouble having fun. Relaxing is difficult for me. I'm not the best company around certain holidays and there isn't a day which goes by that I don't envision or mourn the loss of my career. I spend too much time thinking of how or why it happened and my battle with suicidal ideation. It happens without warning. A car can suddenly park in front of me at an angle. Is it a hit? So I checked my review mirror, nothing. I should be good. I could be driving, stepping off my truck, be on a vacation, or a similar situation that suddenly brings the past to the present and there it is, or it isn't.

The nightmares still come, but I've learned to process them differently now.

I'm a comeback story in progress, and still have a few more *acts* to go.

AFTERWORD

Although there were many emotions, several experiences and numerous lessons that made up this book, it was written with one simple intention, to share with readers and law enforcement officers alike. I wanted others to know that there is life after service. How you live that life is all based on your thought process, associations, what books you decide to pick up and where you choose to spend your time to find purpose post law enforcement.

Due to the trauma and betrayal I had experienced, I needed growth in my life. I had to choose to expand my associations beyond the law enforcement realm, expand my vision through reading, and force myself to spend time in places that brought me value and positioned me for intentional personal growth.

This wasn't a hero book nor were there stories of medals

being awarded, but the children of God with whom I dangerously served undercover operations with performed daily heroic deeds.

"Blessed are the peacemakers, for they will be called children of God."

MATTHEW 5:9

I hope you found their stories, the actions of the guilty, who will intentionally remain nameless, my lessons, mistakes, and my paths, as opportunities for growth because there are no dress rehearsals or operational briefings in this lifetime of ours.

PHOTO GALLERY

State Gang Task Force Arrest Warrant

Vincent T AKA: Jay & Myself "Chino". On the outside we may have come across as well polished drug dealing thugs, but at the core we were highly skilled soldiers & professional lawmen with the ability to bring controlled violence of action if the moment called for it.

Marijuana Seizure. I look like my son in this picture.

Don, Myself & Dan G. After a half million-dollar marijuana reverse operation. May they both rest easy. This job will take your soul one way or another if you allow it.

Walking away from "Chuy" after bringing him a sample kilo of cocaine. A few days later, I made it rain cops on him and his Jamaican money contacts.

"Diablito" bringing me a kilo of cocaine. He was sly like a little fox. Well-connected too.

"Andres el Negro" and I after another undercover reverse drug op. Note the paper sack holding 200k plus in cash and "Angelitos" fancy hardware.

"If you want to be a sheepdog and walk the warrior's path, then you must make a conscious and moral decision every day to dedicate, equip and prepare yourself to thrive in that toxic, corrosive moment when the wolf comes knocking at the door." -LTC. Dave Grossman

Therefore, we knocked first.

Another UC Op. Dudes just loved to bring me money for my weed. Approx 80k here for 150 lbs. Note the load of Mj in the back seat. This op took place right next to and behind a Panda Express. We ran these ops in plain sight and the middle of the day.

Holding 130k from another reverse op

Surveillance photo of me preparing to show my suspect a 2-pound sample of marijuana. He was looking to middle several hundred pounds and wanted to check out my product. He's making sure no one was watching.

Surveillance photo of me bringing a middleman a sample of marijuana in a Home Depot bucket. If you look carefully, he's placing it in his backseat.

1/2

Surveillance photos of "Flaco" showing me a sample of his product. Note the kids innocently walking by not knowing what is even happening.
2/2

Surveillance photo capturing "Flaco" as he tells me he will bring me my product.

"Flaco" returns with the Heroin then flees northbound once SWAT approached. He scaled the wall 50 yds north of us & got away. I suppose it's challenging to beat a determined and heads-up baller.

"Vincent" & "Chino" dangerous boys

Picture of stolen guns purchased during drug buys with some Compton, CA boys. I had to pull back the balaclava to show some face.

Some emails just take you way back. Thank you for the memories "JaySo" & "West Side".

Tio Pancho a Soldier, a gentleman and one heck of a good undercover narc. Thank you for your mentorship. Rest easy Sir!

Hey "Don." He brought us a key of coke and a big gulp! Rest peacefully you legend.

Front & back (top and bottom). I've had this saved in an old photo album that my mother left me since the 6th grade. Sometimes the goal doesn't happen right away, but you are for sure never going to achieve them if you don't write them down someplace. Note the pin hole from it being on a cork board in class and Ms. Brenda Tye's excellent handwriting.

DURESS an award-winning short film I produced highlighting the work of the brave undercover agents I worked with. You can find a link to it on my YouTube.com/Loupimber Please SUBSCRIBE

Pictured here with Jonathan Banks who played Private Detective Mike. I'm thankful for having had the chance to tell Jonathan how he and Ken Wahl inpsired me.

Pictured here with Aaron Paul from AMC's BREAKING BAD.

On the set of BREAKING BAD

Photo from a commercial print ad

Photo from a commercial print ad

Photo from the EWTN Network film, KATERI playing Chief Iowarano. The true story of the first Native American to be named Saint by the Roman Catholic Church. Some know her as Lilly of the Mohawks.

Apparently, I really liked my new ring.

Ft. Bliss, Texas. The Dogs of War

My first step into manhood.

165

What an eye-opening experience this was for me. I'm thankful for every minute of it. The Dogs of War

My Mother, she taught me to never lose faith. May she rest in eternal peace & love.

My dad, Joe, myself, and mother.

MarcAnthony & Nicolle Pimber

I'm extremely proud of my two kids and the Americans that they have become. Their future looks bright.

Lou speaking in Las Vegas.

Reinvention is in-fact a tricky thing. You have to not only pay for it up front, through hard work and perseverance, but you also pay it forward through the mentorship of other people. Lou Pimber pictured here speaking to entrepreneurs in Phoenix, AZ

My wife Rhonda Moretti Pimber and I hosting Belleza Models community Christmas gala event. A charity event to help bring back beautiful confidence.

Lou Pimber and John Maxwell

ABOUT THE AUTHOR

Lou Pimber is a Mexican immigrant, born Luis A Pimber, former U.S. Soldier, Combat Medic, and retired UC law enforcement officer, having served as a member of the Arizona State Gang Task force & HIDTA Counter Narcotics Unit, now turned actor and entrepreneur. Lou retired medically after having sustained career-ending injuries during an Undercover assignment. Lou has been featured in films, television shows like Breaking Bad & Gang Related, and numerous local and national commercials. He has been a nationally sought-out key-note speaker on leadership in business, police undercover work, post-traumatic stress, life post-retirement for law enforcement officers, and the American Dream.

Lou Pimber has a YouTube podcast channel, Lou Pimber Speaks, where he interviews incredible Americans, lawmen & soldiers alike, and business-related content. Lou and his wife, Rhonda Pimber, serve as Presidents of Councils with the PHP Agency, now with multiple offices throughout Arizona & Texas, serving Americans nationally by bringing back free enterprise and hope to families and addressing financial illiteracy, life insurance & retirement income planning. Lou is a true believer in becoming the main character in your life story! Are you living your best life?

Contact Lou if you want to learn how to maximize your growth, leadership potential, and learn about entrepreneurship though his training for adults and children.

www.loupimber.com

instagram.com/loupimber4real
youtube.com/@LouPimber
linkedin.com/in/lou-pimber-715aa145

www.ingramcontent.com/pod-product-compliance
Lightning Source LLC
Chambersburg PA
CBHW062216080426
42734CB00010B/1909